BUDDHA *in the* LANDSCAPE

A Sacred Expression of THAILAND

BUDDHA *in the* LANDSCAPE

A Sacred Expression *of* THAILAND

MARK STANDEN

Text by **JOHN HOSKIN**

Pomegranate

SAN FRANCISCO

TO MY MOTHER MARJORIE, TO LEE, KURT, NAI AND JACK,
AND IN MEMORY OF MY FATHER, DAVID JAMES STANDEN,
WHO TAUGHT ME HOW TO BUILD, AND BOONSONG JANTAVAL,
WHOSE PASSION FOR THAI CULTURE CONTINUES TO INSPIRE.

PUBLISHED BY
Pomegranate Communications, Inc.
Box 6099, Rohnert Park
California 94937

Pomegranate Europe Ltd.
Fullbridge House, Fullbridge
Maldon, Essex CM9 4LE
England

IN ASSOCIATION WITH
Mark Standen Publishing
Company Ltd.

PHOTOGRAPHS:
© 1998 Mark Standen

MAPS:
© 1998 Mark Standen

TEXT:
© 1998 Mark Standen Publishing
Company Ltd.

Pomegranate Catalog No. A936
ISBN 0-7649-0770-0
Library of Congress Catalog Card
Number 98-67146

DESIGN
Annie Miniscloux
Format & Partners Ltd., Bangkok

CARTOGRAPHY
Mark Standen

EDITOR
Keith Hardy

SPECIALIST EDITOR
Achaan Helen Jandamit

EDITORIAL CONSULTANTS
Achaan Jayasaro
Achaan Sujib Punyanubhab
Anurut Vongvanij

CAMERA TECHNICAL SUPPORT
A.V. Camera, Bangkok

FILM PROCESSING
Hollywood E-6, Bangkok

REPRODUCTION
Rainbow Graphic Arts Company Ltd.
Hong Kong

PRINTED AND BOUND BY
Paramount Printing Company Ltd.
Hong Kong

CONTENTS

PHOTOGRAPHER'S PREFACE

The concept for **Buddha in the Landscape** arose while I was travelling in northern Thailand. Noticing a Buddha image located on a small hill, I recalled other images that I had seen in the landscape.

I questioned myself as to why these Buddha statues were built and for what reasons. Within seconds, I had thought of the title of the book, and from a small seed of an idea, **Buddha in the Landscape** started to evolve.

An extraordinary odyssey had begun, a quest that would involve personally driving over 60,000 kilometres throughout the length and breadth of the Kingdom, and which would take over three years from concept to completion of the book.

In those three years I have focused passionately on **Buddha in the Landscape**, appreciating the importance of this publication for Thailand both within the Kingdom and beyond its shores. The impact upon me of these statues of the Lord Buddha has been immeasurable and I can hardly put into words my innermost feelings. But if you, the reader, find beauty, serenity, peace and inspiration within the pages of this book, not only will you be sharing with me a sacred expression of Thailand but also you will understand something of what it has meant to photograph **Buddha in the Landscape**.

Mark Standen
July 19th 1998, Bangkok

Opposite: Luang Pho Phra Ngam, at Wat Khao Phra Ngam, Lop Buri province. **Above:** Photographer Mark Standen on location.

INTRODUCTION

SINCE THE KINGDOM'S FOUNDING in the 13th century, Thailand has drawn distinction from Buddhism. What was embraced as the national religion at Sukhothai, the capital of the sovereign state under which the Thai people were first united, has had a continuous and all-pervading impact on the cultural and social development of the country. It remains today the sacred expression of all that is quintessentially Thai.

Modern city skylines are still characterized by gilded temple spires; early morning activity in towns and villages is set against a background of saffron-robed monks making alms rounds, while Buddha statues gaze serenely from temples, palaces, offices, homes and, not least, the landscape. Thailand is very much the land of the Buddha image, with more statues of the Enlightened One than probably anywhere else in the world.

Vital and visible in daily life, Buddhism is not only professed but practised by nine-tenths of Thailand's 60-million population, and is supported by some 30,000 Buddhist monasteries throughout the Kingdom, a religious community of about 250,000 monks, 100,000 novices and an unrecorded number of nuns. Numbers are maintained both by those who remain permanently in the monkhood and by a constant stream of young Thai men who continue to follow the traditional custom of becoming ordained for a brief period at least once in their lives.

Opposite: The image of Somdet Phra Boromma Trai Lokanat, Nakhon Phanom. **Above:** *Giving alms to monks in the early morning is a daily practice seen throughout Thailand.*

Buddhism is one of the oldest of the world's major religions. In Thailand, the Buddhist calendar predates Christianity by 543 years and Islam by some 1,000 years.

Buddhism is remarkable today for its continuing influence and relevance, in spite of changing cultural and economic patterns as well as a growing trend towards secularism in many parts of the world. Although traditional Buddhist societies, such as that of Thailand, are constantly being challenged by a need to reconcile time-honoured values with the demands of modernization, the relevance of Buddhism is, almost paradoxically, being reinforced.

In his book *Living Buddhism,* Andrew Powell notes that even while many Thais are preoccupied by the pursuit of higher standards of living, 'some well-educated city-dwellers are once again taking to meditation and devoting time to spiritual practice'. The point was underscored at the Fifth International Conference on Thai Studies, held in London in 1993. Concluding a speech on the present-day imbalance between material and spiritual development, Dr. Prawase Wasi reasoned: 'Buddhism represents one of the greatest spiritual resources that can be tapped for the restoration of balanced development as a remedy to world crisis. Thailand, although plagued by crises, still possesses potential spiritual resources which, if appropriately strengthened and harnessed, can contribute to averting human and environmental crisis.'

Popular belief in Buddhism's ongoing importance in Thailand is reflected in the fact that since the late 1980s new Thai Buddhist temples have been built at an average rate of around 170 a year. Moreover, a great many of the large, open-air Buddha images which are the subject of this book are comparatively recent creations, standing not as monuments to a more spiritual past but as modern expressions of what clearly is still held sacred and meaningful.

That Buddhism should remain a source of inspiration among its traditional Asian communities — and for a growing number of people in

The Thai Buddhist temple, with characteristic multi-tiered roof, is Thailand's most widely recognized manifestation of the religion.

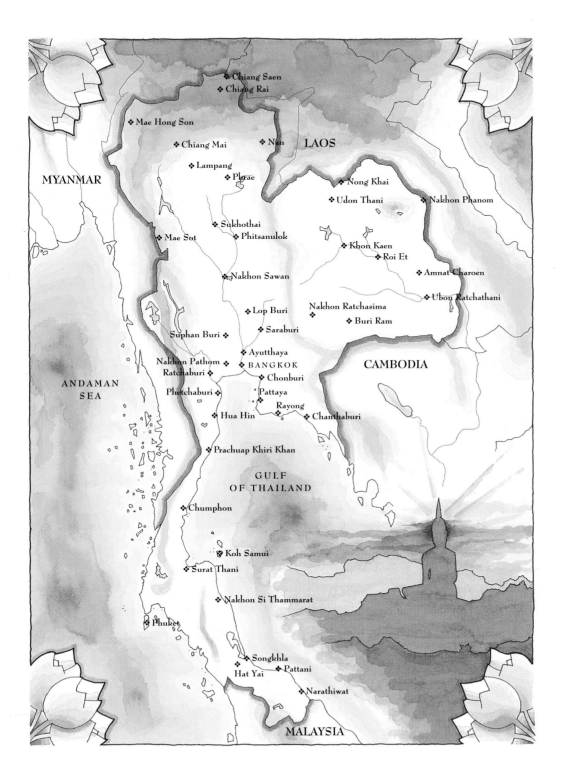

Covering an area of 514,000 sq km, Thailand is bordered by Myanmar (Burma), Laos and Cambodia, which are also Theravada Buddhist countries, and by Malaysia, which is predominantly Muslim.

the West — is due in large part to the religion's basis in reason rather than dogma, and its emphasis on a balance between wisdom and faith. This puts it more in harmony with the modern age, and offers real and practical ways of coping with the pressures of the material world.

Unlike Christianity and Islam, Buddhism does not demand a belief in nor an exclusive allegiance to an all-powerful god. While not ignoring the questions of god and salvation, Buddhism concentrates on an individual's life here and now, and on the inevitable suffering it involves. Its ultimate goal is the cessation of that suffering. In the words of the Buddha, 'I teach only this: suffering and the end of suffering'. The path to the cessation of suffering depends on understanding the way things really are.

Sometimes described as a philosophy rather than a religion, Buddhism is based on clearly formulated ideas. The way to understanding is through a moral code that has long proved simple and appealing. Compassion, honesty, self-control and other attributes of a civilized, productive life are readily embraced. They are also relevant and timeless regardless of the expansion of knowledge and scientific discovery over the ages.

Relevance of a moral code persists because Buddhism places the onus for the end of suffering on the individual, on what he or she can actually do. 'It is a religion of self-help,' writes Buddhist scholar and former monk, Sunthorn Plamintr. 'According to Buddhism, human beings should learn to be self-reliant and to have faith in their own ability. Buddhist philosophy is anthropocentric in its outlook and practical implementation, placing man at the centre of its metaphysical and ethical systems. It is a religion that insists primarily on man's own effort and perseverance to achieve his goals, be they material or spiritual, rather than prayer or wishful thinking.'

However, keeping focused on the path to understanding is often difficult. Accordingly, in order to lend tangible support in the pursuit of its philosophical,

Buddhism offers a path for all, whether monks, nuns or lay people, placing the onus for the end of suffering on the individual.

spiritual and moral teaching, Buddhism also presents a system of symbols and rituals to aid everyday practice and the accumulation of merit. Not least of these tangible supports is the image of the Buddha, which is both a symbol of his teaching and a focal point for devotion.

Nothing symbolizes the essence of Buddhism, its teaching and its practice, more than the Buddha statue. One of the major ways of earning merit has traditionally been the making or commissioning of an image of the Buddha. In the words of the 7th-century Chinese monk, I-Ching, 'Even if a man make an image as small as a grain of barley . . . a special case for good birth is obtained thereby, and will be as limitless as the Seven Seas, and good rewards will last as long as the coming four births. . . .'

Widespread though they have become, images of the Buddha were not the religion's first symbols, and likenesses were not fashioned until several hundred years after the Buddha's death. It is generally accepted that the first figurative images were produced in the early centuries AD at Gandhara, in what is today northwestern Pakistan.

Like previous symbolic representations of the Buddhist faith, such as the *bodhi* tree under which the Buddha achieved enlightenment, or the Wheel which recalls the first sermon that 'set the Wheel of the Law in motion', Buddha images were intended as reminders of the teachings. They were not idols.

The craft of sculpting Buddha statues eventually spread via India and Sri Lanka to Thailand and elsewhere. Theoretically, every image of the Enlightened One is supposed to be a faithful copy, adhering to a convention built up from descriptions recorded in the scriptures. Artists are aware of strict guidelines and are expected to reproduce certain features and attitudes that are traditional and accepted as integral. Therefore, all images display certain common features.

The Wheel of the Law predates Buddha images as a symbol of the religion, recalling the first sermon given by the Buddha.

A standing Buddha displays the abhaya mudra, at Wat Mahathat in Sukhothai, the first Thai capital, founded in the 13th century.

The Buddha is represented as a human being, and likenesses display none of the fantastic anatomy of, say, the multi-limbed forms of certain Hindu gods. And yet the Enlightened One is understood to have been a remarkable personage, bearing 32 major and 80 minor marks which distinguished him from other mortals. Not all of these — the sound of his voice, for instance — lend themselves to visual representation, but a few were established as hallmarks of all Buddha sculptures. Especially characteristic are the *usnisa*, or cranial protuberance, and hair curling in a clockwise direction.

In form, images were confined to just four possible postures — walking, standing, seated (typically cross-legged although, occasionally, as if on a chair in what has become known in the East as 'European' style) and reclining — while the position of the hands was fixed in one of a number of *mudras*, or gestures, signifying certain attitudes associated with the Buddha. Six mudras are specific to Buddha images, of which the most common are the *dhyana* mudra (both hands palm upwards in the lap — seated image); the *bhumisparsa* mudra (left hand in the lap and right hand over the right knee with fingers pointing to the ground — seated image); and *abhaya* mudra (one or both hands raised palm forwards — standing image, although not in every instance).

Standing and seated figures, various in their mudras, are the most widely seen. The reclining statue, less common, usually shows the Buddha lying on his right side, right hand supporting his head — this particular representation depicts him approaching death. The walking figure, a posture inspired by the legend of the Buddha's descent from heaven, after preaching to his mother, is the least common.

Although sculptors adhered to the essential conventions of Buddhist iconography, variations have occurred. In Thailand, for example, numerous schools of sculpture have flourished during different historical periods, resulting in statues displaying distinct stylistic qualities.

The earliest Buddha images found in the country are examples of Indian sculpture from the Gupta (4th-6th centuries) and Pala (8th-11th centuries) schools, but the first style to arise locally, although belonging to a pre-Thai civilization, is that of Dvaravati, which dates from the late 6th or early 7th century to the 11th century. This was the art of the Mon, an ethnic group that settled in central Thailand.

Although partly derived from Indian models, Dvaravati art has distinct features of its own. Images are less massive, more simplified and, in later examples, display indigenous facial characteristics such as a broader nose and thicker lips. There are also differences in the postures; for example, the standing Buddha is styled with both hands performing the mudra, whereas in Indian models the left hand normally holds a fold of the robe.

While Dvaravati held sway over central Thailand, the south was under another powerful kingdom, that of Srivijaya, which was dominant over peninsular Thailand and the Indonesian archipelago from the 8th century to about the end of the 13th. Similarly influenced by Indian forms, with the prototypes gradually being modified by native elements, Srivijaya images differ from those of Dvaravati in that they reflect the *Mahayana* rather than *Theravada* vehicle of Buddhism. *Bodhisattvas* (future Buddhas) were widely portrayed, an outstanding example being a statue of Avalokitesvara discovered in Chaiya in southern Thailand. Dating from the 8th or 9th century and now a treasured possession of the National Museum in Bangkok, the figure is remarkable for its serene and tranquil expression.

Noteworthy in the later Srivijaya period are images of the Buddha in which he is shown seated beneath a *naga* (mythical serpent). One particular late 12th-century example, while typifying the late Srivijaya style, also illustrates the beginning of Khmer influence, especially in the form of the naga heads and in the square face of the Buddha. Khmer style, sometimes

The naga protects the Buddha, as recalled in a story of when the Buddha was meditating during a storm, and is often featured in late Srivijaya- and Khmer-style images.

referred to as Lop Buri art, is the third and last of the major pre-Thai schools of Buddha sculpture, generally dated from the 11th to the 13th centuries. Much of the area now defined by Thailand's national borders was at one time encompassed by the Khmer empire and, in particular, the eastern and central part of the country was punctuated with many provincial centres of importance, of which Lop Buri was one.

Lop Buri Buddha images were either carved in stone or cast in bronze, and typical characteristics are the cranial protuberance, modified into three rows of lotus petals, and a lotus bud halo. As Mahayana Buddhism was dominant with the Khmers, statues of the Buddha in royal attire were common at this time. Such apparel included a diadem and many types of jewellery of which only a selection was generally depicted on any one image, earrings and necklaces being most common.

By the 13th century the power of the Khmers was waning whereas the Thais, who continued to migrate from southern China, most historians believe, were gaining strength. They established their first sovereign kingdom at Sukhothai in c. 1250. It was here that Thai art had its first and arguably finest flowering; the most beautiful and most original Buddha images date from this period. Influences from Dvaravati, Khmer and Sri Lankan art (the latter reviving and strengthening the impact of Theravada Buddhism) were combined with indigenous genius to produce something unique.

Sukhothai images were more stylized than anything built before, with a greater fluidity in the line of the body and an uncanny degree of serenity and spirituality in the facial features. Key characteristics are a tall flame halo, small haircurls, oval face, arched eyebrows, hooked nose and a smiling expression. Also, the artists interpreted descriptions of the Buddha as given in *Pali* texts, tending to stress particular features such as the cranial protuberance, long arms and flat-soled feet with projecting heels.

At the ancient capital of Sukhothai, Buddhism was embraced as the national faith, reflected in both the architecture and sculpture of the period.

Statues in the seated posture were popular, but the greatest triumph of the Sukhothai artists, and perhaps the highest artistic achievement of all in Thai sculpture, was the walking Buddha. This posture had appeared before but only in carved relief; it was a Thai innovation to produce walking images in the round.

Not only was originality achieved, it was achieved in a most stunning fashion with the artists brilliantly capturing their subject in a frozen moment of walking with one heel raised and the other foot firmly planted on the ground; one arm swinging freely at the side with the other expressing an abhaya mudra. The aesthetic quality of these Buddha images has never been surpassed.

At roughly the same time as Sukhothai was consolidating its kingdom, the Thais in the north of the country were united in the Lanna kingdom, the capital of which, Chiang Mai, was founded in 1296. Its school of art is generally referred to as Chiang Saen style, named after the town which earlier was a power centre of the region and where a number of images of great merit have been found.

Chiang Saen art falls into two basic groups, early and late. The images of the former exemplify Indian Pala styles which were likely inherited from Haripunchai (present-day Lamphun), an offshoot of the Mon Dvaravati kingdom which was conquered by Lanna. Distinctive characteristics are a halo in the form of a lotus bud, round face, prominent chin and a stout body with a well-developed chest.

The later period, at its height during the reign of the Lanna King Tilokaraja (1442-1487), coincided with the blossoming of Theravada Buddhism in the north, and shows both Sukhothai and Sri Lankan influences in the flame halo, oval face and more slender body of the Buddha images. As with Sukhothai art, seated statues are common but the Chiang Saen examples differ in that they are usually mounted on lotus flower pedestals.

A 15th-century walking Buddha displayed at The Ramkhamhaeng National Museum, Sukhothai. This form is widely regarded as expressing the finest flowering of Thai Buddhist sculpture.

In art, as well as in politics, the kingdoms of Lanna and Sukhothai eventually became subordinate to Ayutthaya, a younger Thai kingdom, which consolidated its power in the Chao Phraya river basin. The sculpture of this period is divided into two categories, that of U-Thong, also known as early Ayutthaya (12th-15th centuries), and Ayutthaya proper, which lasted until the mid-18th century.

U-Thong images passed through stages when Dvaravati, Lop Buri and Sukhothai styles in turn dominated, though they are essentially typified by a square face and a stern expression. Even those most strongly marked by the impact of Sukhothai models are less stylized than the originals and show a more human anatomy.

In the Ayutthaya style proper the heritage of Sukhothai came to outweigh that of the Khmers, although the U-Thong form never completely vanished, but the Buddha images of this period are scarcely comparable to the achievements of Sukhothai's Golden Age. In particular, faces tended to be lifeless and, in general, artists were content to copy. However, some distinction was achieved in the late Ayutthaya period when crowned Buddhas, or Buddhas in royal attire, were popular but even here the decoration is more distinguished than the portrayal of the features and characteristics of the Buddha.

Ayutthaya fell to the Burmese in 1767 and the following — and current — period of Thai art, that of Rattanakosin, or Bangkok, dates from the establishment of the present Thai capital in 1782. During the first reign of the current Chakri dynasty very few new Buddha images were produced; temples were decorated with statues, generally in Sukhothai, U-Thong and Ayutthaya styles, that were collected from around the country. Some of the best examples of these can be seen today in the galleries of Bangkok's Wat Po.

The chedis of Wat Phra Sri Sanphet are among the finest surviving temple ruins of ancient Ayutthaya, the Thai capital from 1350 to 1767.

In the reigns of King Rama II (1809-1824) and King Rama III (1824-1851), crowned Buddhas were produced but, as with those of Ayutthaya, more emphasis was given to the decoration than the facial expression. Yet one masterpiece does date from the reign of King Rama III — the giant statue of the reclining Buddha enshrined at Wat Po. Its massive size tends to overpower more aesthetic considerations but it is nonetheless an extremely serene image.

Increasingly in the Rattanakosin period artists have tended to produce more lifelike images and while certain traditional characteristics are shown, such as the flame halo and extended earlobes, the overall effect is that of a more humanized figure. A fine example of this is the standing Buddha, made in 1957 to commemorate the 2,500th anniversary of Buddhism, which is today housed in the National Museum at Bangkok.

Outside of their historical moment, styles of sculpture have been variously favoured according to the personal preferences of the patrons who commissioned them. Presently, Sukhothai-style images tend to be the most popular due in part, as Thai art historian Dr. Piriya Krairiksh points out, to 'the political climate of the time which sees Sukhothai as the fount of Thai national identity, and the apogee of Thai artistic endeavours'.

To talk of sculptural styles often raises the question of aesthetics. Historically, even skilled and dedicated artists responsible for crafting images sought neither self-expression nor the achievement of an original work of art. Yet it is equally true in present-day estimation that numerous images of the Buddha are masterpieces of sculpture, possessing a high and certain aesthetic value.

In explaining this apparent contradiction, one art historian has suggested that however potent a particular image's magical power might be, it 'would not have achieved such an illustrious history had it not had superior aesthetic

The style of Buddhist sculpture in the Rattanakosin period is exemplified by the huge reclining Buddha located at Wat Phra Chetuphon, also known as Wat Po, in Bangkok.

quality'. Many other images would likewise not have survived the ravages of time 'were it not for their enduring aesthetic value'.

Appreciation of beauty may not have been a sculptor's conscious aim, but its aesthetic value has served in the lasting power of the Buddha image. Thai artists throughout the Kingdom's long history have excelled in the production of these sacred images. Although Buddhist sculpture is primarily devotional, that has not inhibited the perfecting of technique.

Regardless of sculptural styles and although not being worshipped as idols, all images lend physical substance to the practice of the religion, and Thais pay enormous respect to Buddha statues. Kneeling in front of an image, they raise their hands, palms together and, in a very formal version of the traditional *wai* greeting, bow the head low three times in homage to the Buddha, his teachings, and the spiritual community of monks and nuns known as the *Sangha*. They make offerings of flowers, candles and incense, and many press little squares of gold leaf onto the statue.

In practice, popular devotion may involve some belief in supernatural powers possessed by the Buddha. Images may then act as less remote and more accessible physical substitutes for the person of the Buddha, providing tangible support to Buddhists in their practice.

A rational explanation for such belief in the miraculous powers of an image is that a potent symbol reminding one of the Buddha's teaching can have a positive psychological impact. It may stimulate a thought process in the devotee whereby, for example, fear of evil spirits is expelled, inducing peace of mind.

Although considered a human being and not a deity, the Buddha is generally credited with certain supernatural powers such as clairvoyance, a knowledge of past and future lives, and the ability to perform miracles. Such powers are traditionally summed up by the *teja*, the 'fiery energy', which the

Placing tiny squares of gold leaf on an image is one of the traditional ways in which people pay respect to the Buddha.

Enlightened One reputedly possessed in abundance, and which is symbolized in the flame-shaped halo depicted in statues of one style or other.

In imagemaking, Buddha statues are ritualistically imbued with the teja, activated during the ceremony devised for the consecration of a new image. At this time the spirit of the Buddha is invited to reside in the new likeness.

Once consecrated, an image transcends the material. It is no longer just a physical object and is considered as a living being possessed of an inner spirit that is its own. In the past, the strength of such belief was witnessed in the laws of ancient Ayutthaya which counted sacrilegious acts against a Buddha image as heinous crimes. To cut off the head of a Buddha statue was murder and scraping off gold leaf was equivalent to skinning a person alive; such crimes incurred severe punishment.

If today's laws are less harsh, the same principle is adhered to and desecration of a Buddha image is an indictable offence. Not many years ago, some foreign tourists were arrested after holiday snapshots developed locally pictured them posing on an ancient Buddha statue.

A further example of the care bestowed on images is illustrated by the royal practice of restoring statues damaged or broken during the destruction wrought by war. An inscription records how, in the late 18th century, the ruler of the northern Thai Lanna kingdom performed such an act because 'he thought of the old images, lying broken in the field and forest, neglected and exposed to sun and rain; and he took pity on them in his heart'.

Similarly, one of the earliest acts of King Rama I, after he had founded Bangkok as the new Thai capital, was to send his brother, the Wang Na Prince, throughout the land to collect images that had been toppled during the war with the Burmese, or which lay neglected at the sites of the Kingdom's ancient cities. In this way more than 1,200 statues were brought to Bangkok and distributed among the several monasteries that recently had been built in the new capital.

Old or new, irrespective of their condition, images of the Buddha are deemed sacred, commanding respect.

An interesting footnote to the practice of restoring Buddha images in the modern age is the problem it creates for archaeologists. When an ancient site is being restored a damaged statue should, from the art historian's point of view, be left as it is, any missing parts being merely regrettable. For the Buddhist, however, it is an act of respect to make a new head, or whatever, in order to restore the image to its complete 'personal' self, regardless of whether this might detract from the statue's aesthetic value.

On an everyday level, Buddha images were, and continue to be, treated with great personal respect. They are presented with offerings on special ceremonial occasions and, during *Songkran*, the traditional Thai New Year, statues both in temples and private homes are ritually bathed.

The Thais' attitude towards a Buddha image being imbued with the life of the Enlightened One is perhaps most emphatically expressed in the language and terminology used. When speaking of an image the correct pronoun is not the equivalent of 'it' but, rather, an honorific loosely translating as 'His Holiness'. Also, a Buddha statue is never taken or shipped from one place to another; it is always 'invited to proceed'. Remarkably, given their vast commercial output in Thailand, Buddha images are not regarded as being 'bought', but only 'leased'. That is because a Buddha image should never be considered as anyone's sole property, but only a temporary possession.

The teja of a particular image may be considered especially powerful, to the extent of imparting miraculous powers. In this way certain images have become legendary by their reputed ability to come unscathed through all kinds of catastrophes and mishaps. The Emerald Buddha, enshrined at Bangkok's Wat Phra Keo, is the palladium of the nation largely because it has survived various troubles and lengthy travels in its long history, and is thus considered to be exceptionally powerful. Another notable example of a Buddha image that has survived extreme circumstances, and is thus considered to be miraculously

The huge restored Buddha at Wat Sri Chum, Sukhothai, may originally have been constructed to be viewed in the open, only later being enclosed by a mondop.

endowed, is the presiding statue at Wat Pho Chai in the northeastern town of Nong Khai. As legend has it, the gold statue floated ashore after the raft on which it was being transported was wrecked in the Mekong River.

While some statues may be popularly considered to possess supernatural powers, all Buddha images are sacred and accorded supreme respect by Thais. Above all they are desired by the people as a tangible manifestation of their devotion and as a support to the practice of the faith.

Although the large statues which stand alone in the Thai landscape are no different in essence from other representations of the Enlightened One, certain distinctions are worth noting. Unlike many Buddha images found in temples, some of those seen in the landscape may appear to lack clear aesthetic value. This, of course, in no way detracts from their function as religious symbols, but it does mean that anyone more familiar with historic Buddhas, those characteristic of the various Thai schools of sculpture, may find some of the large statues hard to define stylistically. Only the finest of the open-air Buddhas display any distinct style and many draw on mixed influences, perhaps most commonly from the popular Sukhothai school.

Any such lack of clear artistic distinction is in part due to the vast majority of the landscape statues being modern creations (constructed usually within the last 50 years, during which time there has been little stylistic innovation). Moreover, the materials of brick or reinforced concrete, as well as the huge proportions, make successful creative sculpture more difficult to achieve compared to smaller, cast-bronze images.

Rising to a height of 15 metres or more (sometimes much more), Buddha images in the landscape are imposing in themselves, but their location is also an important consideration, amounting almost to an attribute of the image. As well as a prominent and often elevated location, the natural beauty of a setting and the sense of calm and serenity arising from physical isolation

Changing the robes of the highly revered gold image known as Luang Pho Phra Sai Buddha, at Wat Pho Chai, Nong Khai.

are also important elements to be considered in the overall design and function of the statue.

Other factors may also affect the siting of an image. Sometimes a statue may be built in a park where people come to enjoy natural beauty, or constructed where a natural formation in the landscape has some particular significance such as a likeness to the Buddha's footprint. Alternatively, an image may be placed at a prominent point along a road or pathway to offer good luck to travellers, or in the pure natural setting of a forest.

The underlying reason for constructing a Buddha in the landscape is usually the same as for most images — mainly to serve as a reminder of the teachings. But various other purposes are often fulfilled, too. Aiding protection of the natural environment, a form of merit-making, a means of exorcism at a place felt to be in some way evil or unlucky, a comfort during sickness; these and other functions may express an individual's or community's aim in commissioning a statue.

Although there is generally a commonality of function and purpose between Buddha images, those in the landscape do have a vital distinction which reinforces an aspect of Buddhist thought less obviously represented by some other images. The point is well summed up by an abbot of a temple near the northeastern town of Nakhon Phanom. Asked what a Buddha statue in the open meant to him, he replied: 'The image is a model of the Buddha and a symbol of Buddhism. It is a reminder that the Lord Buddha lived most of his life out in the open with nature. While everything around him was constantly changing, this did not change the Lord Buddha. When it was hot, he was not hot; when it was cold, he was not cold. This illustrates that the Lord Buddha's mind was constant and at peace, undisturbed and unchanged by events around him. Thus the image in the landscape reminds us that if we can keep our minds like this, then changes outside of ourselves will not change us inside.'

A temple mural painting at Wat Noi Pho Kham, Nakhon Phanom, shows devotees bearing candles ascending the hill to pay homage to a large Buddha in the landscape.

There is a parallel between images of the Buddha in the landscape and temple murals which typically show the Enlightened One in a natural setting, with depictions of forests, mountains, lakes, wild animals and similar scenes. The huge statues in the open emphasize this point not only through their large and powerful form, but also by their location in a natural environment.

That the majority of large Buddhas seen today in the Thai landscape are of comparatively modern construction (and continue to be built) seems to suggest that the phenomenon is a recent one. There is, however, evidence to indicate the practice is of ancient tradition and that many of the huge statues now enshrined in temples originally stood in the open. Some art historians believe this to be the case with certain images preserved at Sukhothai, while historical evidence clearly shows that the statue of Luang Pho To, now enshrined in Wat Phanan Choeng at Ayutthaya, formerly stood uncovered and highly visible. A sign erected at the site reads: 'A historical chronicle states that this gilded stucco image was made in AD 1324, 26 years before the founding of Ayutthaya as the capital of the Thai Kingdom in AD 1350. Originally the Buddha image was exposed to the elements of nature in accordance with Thai tradition, where no covering structure was made over a large statue so that the magnificence of the image could well be admired from any angle, as well as from any visible distance.'

Travelling through Thailand today reveals a surprising number of Buddhas erected in the open. Ironically, many people miss them, perhaps because often they are more accustomed to appreciating images in a temple context. Certainly, although the Buddhist temple has become the country's most widely recognized manifestation of its religion, the Buddha in the landscape nonetheless is a most powerful reminder of the teachings, wonderfully preserving an ancient tradition which remains to this day a remarkable and sacred expression of Thailand.

Enshrined in Wat Phanan Choeng, Ayutthaya, the large Buddha statue known as Luang Pho To was originally built in the open to be viewed from any visible distance.

THE NORTH

Chiang Saen
Chiang Rai
Mae Hong Son
Chiang Mai
Lampang
Nan
Phrae

Bangkok

THE NORTH OF THAILAND is an area of picturesquely rugged uplands, characterized by high forested hills, including the Kingdom's highest point, Doi Inthanon, which rises to 2,565 metres. Traversing the highlands are four principal rivers — the Ping, the Wang, the Yom and the Nan — all of which flow roughly north to south. The region's northern border meets those of two neighbouring countries — Laos to the east and Myanmar to the west.

Chiang Mai, the capital of the North, and most other major settlements are clustered in the fertile valleys, where rice is cultivated along with a variety of fruits, vegetables and flowers that benefit from the region's fairly temperate climate. Traditionally, the upland areas have been occupied by various groups of hill tribes, people of distinct ethnic origin who continue for the most part to maintain their separate lifestyles. In the past, the principal crop of the northern hills was the opium poppy but its cultivation has been drastically reduced as a combined result of royal crop substitution programmes and certain other benefits such as improved education facilities, better medical services and advancements in general social welfare provision.

The economic boom of the late 1980s and early 1990s has inevitably brought change to the North, and Chiang Mai is no longer the quaint backwater it once was. Yet many sleepy highland settlements still retain a character all their own, hidden in valleys surrounded by timeless hills.

Opposite: A standing Buddha seen in the morning mist amid typical northern scenery of fertile fields and rolling hills.

A modern seated Buddha occupies a site on Doi Kham,

near Chiang Mai, replacing an earlier image built in 1933.

The sun setting between the wooded hills highlights the prominence and serenity of the Buddha on Doi Kham.

Previous pages: The seated Buddha at Wat Doi Saket, Chiang Mai. **Opposite and above:** The statue, easily visible from afar, forms part of a hilltop temple complex and was built to commemorate the 60th birthday of Her Majesty Queen Sirikit.

Opposite: *The face of the Buddha at Wat Doi Saket displays a blend of classical styles, while* **(above)** *the right hand expresses the vitarka mudra, indicating reasoning or explanation.*

A seated Buddha, reached by a naga-flanked staircase and
draped with ceremonial robes, shows the Burmese influence
which is commonly found in the sculpture and architecture
of the far northwestern town of Mae Hong Son.

Opposite: Wat Tha Ton, with its two large Buddhas in the open, one gold and one white, dominates the west bank of the Mae Kok river at Tha Ton town, close to the border with Myanmar. The gold Buddha **(above)**, on the higher level, is seated beneath a multi-headed naga, or mythical serpent.

Previous pages: *Details of the two Buddhas at Wat Tha Ton.* **Above and opposite:** *Near Chiang Rai, located on private land, this standing Buddha featuring an honorific parasol was built as a focal point for a meditation centre.*

*Occupying a landscaped setting filled with a complex arrangement of statuary (**opposite**), the image at Wat Phra That Chom Mok Kaeo represents the Buddha's first sermon, given to his first five disciples (**above**).*

Many young teak trees have been planted around the image at Wat Phra That Chom Mok Kaeo to recreate the forest setting in which the historic Buddha delivered his first sermon. The landscaping also serves as a conservation exercise.

Grouped in the outer perimeter are statues of celestial
beings paying respect and listening to the Buddha.
The mass of statuary and the surroundings in general
have the effect of emphasizing the commanding presence
of the Buddha.

The newly completed Buddha statue is blessed in the
Chalong Sompot ceremony, where devotees circumambulate
the image three times in a candlelit procession *(above)*, and
are addressed by the commissioning abbot *(opposite)*.

An image in Chiang Saen is shown (**above**) with the robes being changed. **Opposite:** This Buddha, portrayed in a typically serene atmosphere amid a leafy grove, evokes the calmness and emphasis on nature implicit in Buddhism.

Previous pages: A Buddha seated in European style depicts the legend of the monkey and the elephant (see additional captions). **Opposite and above:** The hilltop Buddha near Mae Chan dominates the landscape.

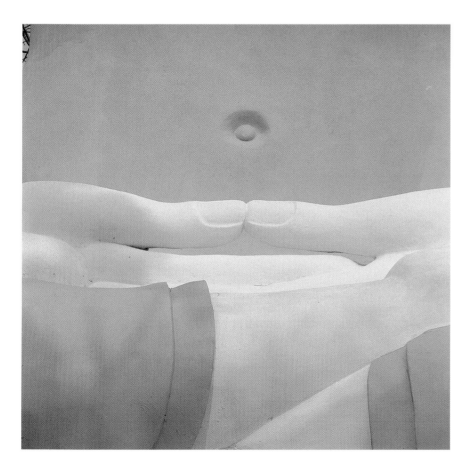

Shown in greater detail, this Buddha near Mae Chan expresses the dhyana mudra, signifying meditation, and was commissioned in order to allay local fears that the site was occupied by evil spirits. Until the Buddha was built, villagers would rarely venture up the hill.

Visible from afar, this reclining Buddha at Mae Chan was built to remind the local community of Buddhist values.

*This prominent hillside Buddha, displaying the varada
mudra, signifying the granting of gifts or favours, faces
the small town of Thoeng, and serves to attract devotees
to the temple at the hill's summit.*

Rickety bamboo scaffolding covers an image in the final stages of completion, near the village of Chiang Muan.

Great attention is paid to the painting of the Buddha's eyes, an integral part of giving life to the statue.

The blue sky and green trees accentuate this white
Buddha near Phan, giving added impact to the sculpture.

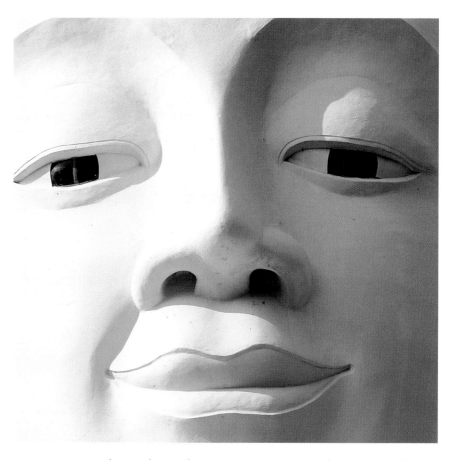

The mudra, indicating reasoning or explanation, and the face of this Buddha exemplify the attention paid to detail in the construction and final finish of the statue.

Appearing in stark solitude, almost as if floating, this standing Buddha near Phan is a perfect example of the blend between nature and spirituality which makes images seen in the landscape such dramatic, powerful forms.

With its high hills, the North offers lush, dominant
locations for Buddha images in the open.

Silhouetted at dusk, the standing bronze Buddha at Wat Analayo, Phayao, is among the tallest bronze images in Thailand at 25 metres.

Offerings, placed at the feet of the Buddha at Wat
Analayo **(above)**, are regularly made to this image
which is highly revered. At the entrance to the courtyard
surrounding the Buddha **(opposite)**, a tree has been left
in place in line with the temple's concern for conservation.

Previous pages: The Chalong Sompot blessing ceremony
at Wat Analayo, presided over by H.R.H. Crown Prince
Vajiralongkorn. The occasion featured a spectacular
firework display. **Above:** At Wat Phra That Nong Chan,
near the village of Song in Phrae province, the Buddha
image is set in a rural scene of agricultural activity.

In spite of its low-lying site, the Buddha image at Wat Phra That Nong Chan stands out above the treetops.

In addition to their prime function as reminders of the teachings, Buddha statues in the open often denote from afar the location of a temple, as shown here in this panoramic view of the image and landscape at Wat Phra That Nong Chan.

The Life of the Lord Buddha

The Buddha, meaning 'The Enlightened One', or 'The Awakened One', was born Siddhattha Gotama around the year 623 BC (563 BC according to some sources) in what is now southern Nepal. His father was King Suddhodana, his mother Queen Maya, rulers of the small kingdom of the Sakyas, and the young Prince Siddhattha was brought up amid the ease and luxury of a royal court.

His father expected that Siddhattha would eventually succeed him although, at the baby prince's naming ceremony, *Brahman* priests had predicted he would become either a world leader or a great religious teacher. Accordingly, King Suddhodana, knowing that it would be the experience of the hard, painful things in life which would turn his son's mind towards religion, did everything in his power to ensure Siddhattha was sheltered from harsh realities.

Showing signs of greatness from an early age, Siddhattha was kind, compassionate and possessed of great wisdom. In time he married a young princess, Yasodhara, and was later to have a son named Rahula. He seemed set to become a worthy successor to his father's throne.

However, on rare excursions away from his royal home, beginning during his youth, he visited four gardens, each on a different occasion. At each, he witnessed a sight for the first time that, severally, would completely change the course of his life. The sights which he saw were those of an old man, a sick man, a corpse and an itinerant monk.

Siddhattha was greatly shocked at the unexpected exposure to human misery he encountered with the first three sights; becoming inspired by the example of the monk, who reflected compassion, and who had forsaken all worldly possessions, Siddhattha resolved to seek understanding of life and of man's suffering. Soon after the birth of his son, he left the palace secretly, believing that if he were to remain there his love for his newborn child would bind him to the secular life. At that time he was 29 years old.

Siddhattha discarded his fine royal clothes in favour of humble apparel. He studied under the two greatest teachers of his day but was unable to find answers to many of his questions. He departed to seek the truth elsewhere. Meeting five ascetics, diligent in their practice, he accompanied them for the next six years, following a path of asceticism so austere that his body wasted away.

Siddhattha began to realize that he should abandon this path of extreme austerity and seek a 'Middle Way' of moderation and meditation. In the *suttas*, or Buddhist holy writings, the reason for his abandonment of asceticism is given by the Buddha himself. He recalled an experience as a child when, attending a ceremony, his mind had become intensely concentrated on his breathing process. He remembered how he had begun to meditate, freeing himself from worldly thoughts and desires, experiencing true happiness, oblivious of the scene around him.

When Siddhattha recalled this childhood memory, he pondered its meaning. He felt that if he were to continue on an austere path, he would probably die before attaining enlightenment. On the other hand, if he were to immerse himself in a life of desire, his energy would not be well enough directed to attain inner peace and happiness. He came to see that the optimum method of practice was a 'Middle Way' of moderation. When Siddhattha told the five ascetics of his decision, they departed, not understanding why he wanted to abandon his austere practices.

Siddhattha began to beg for sustenance and, becoming better nourished, started to regain his strength. Soon, fully recovered, both physically and mentally, he felt prepared and ready for enlightenment. At the town of Bodhgaya in northern India, Siddhattha sat alone beneath a bodhi, or bo, tree to meditate, determined not to rise until he had gained enlightenment, which he attained on the night of the full moon.

Now, at the age of 35, Siddhattha became known as the Buddha; shortly after his enlightenment he started to preach. His teachings came to be known as the *Dhamma*. These teachings form the core of the Buddhist religious system, and the Buddha taught solely on the basis of what he had come to understand for himself, without in any way subscribing to the notion of a divine grace or supernatural power.

In the beginning, the Buddha was reluctant to teach others what he had discovered, thinking it might prove too difficult for them to understand; but he realized there were some who could and, using supernormal powers which he had developed during his long training, he mentally searched for those who would comprehend his message. At Sarnath, near Varanasi, he met the five ascetics again and it was to them that he then delivered his first sermon. They became his first disciples.

The Buddha spent the subsequent years of his long life — he died in his 80th year — teaching around the central region of the Ganges plain, gathering a large number of followers from all walks of life.

Disciples of the Buddha were encouraged to accept complete responsibility for their thoughts and actions on a path to spiritual growth that was not only a religious experience but also a way of life. Furthermore, the Buddha made clear that he considered monastic life as providing the most conducive environment for the study, practice, realization, preservation and propagation of the Dhamma. So the monastic community known as the Sangha was founded, in which ordained followers entered into the practice of living disciplined lives and in which they sought freedom from suffering.

Thus were established the fundamentals of the Buddhist faith — the *Triratna*, or 'threefold jewel', known also as the Triple Gem, which refers to: the Buddha, the Enlightened One; the Dhamma, literally 'the truth within the teachings' or, more superficially, 'the texts containing the teachings'; and the Sangha which, today, means the spiritual community or, more specifically, the ordained community of monks and nuns, although originally it meant the community of those of who have entered 'the Stream of Enlightenment'.

Although Buddhism would become an organized religion centred on the Sangha, the Buddha emphasized self-reliance, a message given in a famous speech shortly before his death: 'Therefore . . . be islands unto yourselves,' he instructed. 'Be your own refuge. Take yourself to no external refuge. Hold fast to the Dhamma as to an island. Hold fast as a refuge to the Truth. . . .'

At the end of his life, when he was at Kusinara, the Buddha is said to have prepared for death by lying down on his right side, right hand supporting his head. Remaining serene, he addressed his *bhikkhus* (disciples) for the last time, saying: 'Then, bhikkhus, I address you now. Transient are conditioned things. Try to accomplish your aim with diligence.' He then entered into meditation until *parinibbana* (his final passing away) took place.

By this time, the Buddha's teachings had taken root in what had become, as described by one Thai Buddhist scholar, 'a spiritual revolution, a large-scale social reform, and a phenomenon unique in the history of religions'.

Although no written record of the Dhamma was made until more than 200 years after the Buddha's death, Buddhism was spread by word of mouth throughout the Indian subcontinent, west into what are now Pakistan and Afghanistan, south to Sri Lanka, and east to Burma, Thailand and the rest of the Orient. Although not now widely practised in India, the land of its origin, Buddhism experienced a period of expansion which lasted 1,500 years. Today, the number of Buddhists in the world is estimated to exceed 300 million.

Over the centuries, a vast literature of myths, legends and stories about the Buddha has been written, relating both to his last life and to his previous lives. It is, however, the example of Siddhattha Gotama, his enlightenment and his subsequent teachings which are the essence of Buddhism.

Opposite: A mural painting of the Buddha gaining enlightenment after meditating beneath a bodhi tree. **Above:** *A scene depicting the death of the Buddha.*

THE NORTHEAST

THAILAND'S LARGEST TOPOGRAPHICAL REGION, covering about one-third of the country's land mass, the Northeast is bordered to the north and east by Laos, the two countries being separated by the Mekong river, and to the south by Cambodia. The landscape is a semiarid plateau with wooded mountains in the northwest, the last remnants of the region's former dense forest cover.

Although containing about one-third of Thailand's population and some of the nation's largest cities such as Khon Kaen, Nakhon Ratchasima and Ubon Ratchathani, the Northeast is intensely rural, its urban centres serving primarily as commercial hubs for the more characteristic village communities. Due to poor soil and unreliable rains, however, agriculture is largely reduced to the level of subsistence farming.

The Northeast preserves rural customs to a marked degree. The people speak their own local dialects, have their own distinctly spiced cuisine and their own handicrafts, notably hand-woven, tie-dyed matmi silk. They typically follow agrarian lifestyles rooted in tradition and dictated by the annual cycle of the farming seasons.

With an enduring agricultural focus, local culture, as seen in music, folk dances and legends, is better preserved than elsewhere in Thailand. This is most readily witnessed in the many time-honoured festivals which punctuate an otherwise arduous annual round of rice cultivation.

Opposite: Nestled in the hills near Pak Chong, Nakhon Ratchasima province, a seated Buddha marks the gateway to the Northeast.

*Previous pages: A long, straight approach from the main highway heightens the presence of the Pak Chong Buddha. The statue can be seen from many angles, such as at a distance across cornfields **(above)** and from the approach staircase **(above right)**. The image is backed by the lush greenery of the hill **(opposite)**.*

Previous pages: With the Buddha at Pak Chong in the background, cultivated roses are being gathered.
Opposite: A Buddha-crowned hill overlooks rice paddies. Located in the heart of the Northeast, in Khon Kaen province, the image is backed by Ubonrat reservoir *(above)*.

Above and opposite: Fashioned with the varada mudra
and sitting on a lotus base, the Buddha at Ubonrat is
a huge structure, rising to a height of 40 metres above
its already prominent location.

The hilltop Buddha at Ubonrat is approached by a steep staircase flanked by naga balustrades **(opposite)**, while **(above)** the Buddha's supportive structure features decorative windows for a room that is contained within.

Previous pages: *A natural stone bridge provides the perfect site to shelter a reclining Buddha image at Ubonrat, Khon Kaen province.* **Above and opposite:** *Caves are often deemed sacred places for their natural beauty and frequently enshrine Buddha images as here at Erawan Cave, Nong Bua Lam Phu.*

*With finely sculpted details of the hands (**above**) and a painted face (**above left**), the Buddha sits in the entrance of Erawan Cave from where there are panoramic views of the northeastern landscape (**opposite**).*

In a stunning rural setting, near Erawan Cave, a gold painted Buddha is shown in the distance **(opposite)** and shown overlooking the landscape **(above)**. The image sits at the foot of a hill, close to the main road, offering good luck to travellers.

Unlike most statues built on or amid a natural elevation
to look outwards, this image in Nong Bua Lam Phu
province was constructed to face back towards the hill.

*Set in beautiful rolling hills (**opposite**), this gold painted Buddha in Nong Bua Lam Phu commands a striking presence, particularly against a backdrop of the rising moon (**above**).*

On the fertile Mekong flood plains, in Nong Khai
province, where cash crops are extensively cultivated,
an unusual Buddha image, with a nine-tiered honorific
parasol, sits in stark isolation.

Covered with small brown mosaic tiles, this magnificent
Buddha in Nakhon Phanom extensively details Chiang
Saen, Sukhothai and Rattanakosin stylistic influences.
The image expresses a fine example of the bhumisparsa
mudra, which signifies 'calling the Earth to witness the
subduing of Mara'.

*Previous pages: In the grounds of a temple school near Mukdahan, young monks diligently clean their alms bowls in front of a sculpted scene of the Buddha preaching his first sermon. **Above and right:** The main statue is seated in front of an ornate 'Wheel of the Law'.*

This statue expresses a variant of the dhammacakra mudra, signifying setting the Wheel of the Law in motion, and symbolizes the first sermon preached by the Buddha. This particular example shows the right hand index finger pointing to the left hand middle finger, representing the Middle Path, or Middle Way.

This Buddha at Amnat Charoen has two smaller images at the base for people to apply gold leaf.

Reputedly the world's tallest freestanding Buddha statue, at 67.85 metres high, this image provides a focal point not only at its location in Roi Et town but also when viewed from much of the surrounding countryside.

Previous pages and above: *The Roi Et Buddha rises high above the town and the temple's adjacent buildings.*

Although a huge statue, the Roi Et image perfectly captures the essential serenity of the Lord Buddha.

Above: A Buddha statue in Kalasin province sits atop a hill which has been designated a natural park. *Opposite:* A few other supporting sculptures, including that of a tiger, have been added to the site, emphasizing the importance of nature.

This Buddha image situated near Buri Ram town
is pictured during and after cleaning and repainting.

A Buddha in Surin province occupies one of the few hills
in an otherwise flat landscape characteristic of the region.

The flat land surrounding this Buddha in Surin is used to cultivate rice.

Previous pages, opposite and above: *The Buddha in Surin was built to replace an old temple which stood on the site originally. The image maintains the sacred meaning of the hill which was once volcanic and has long been revered by the local people.*

The Teachings of the Lord Buddha

Although it is one of the world's most widely practised faiths, Buddhism differs from most major religions in that it is not centred on a required belief in the existence of a god but is, essentially, a rational philosophy based on the knowledge and understanding of the way things really are.

This fundamental truth, realized by the Buddha, and which he subsequently relayed to others, is known as the Dhamma, or the teachings of the Buddha, which is the second component of the Triple Gem (the first being the Buddha, the third being the Sangha). The Dhamma is meant for everyone without distinction of any kind, whether in the monastic order or in the lay community.

The Buddha's insight into ultimate reality is embodied in the 'Four Noble Truths', as outlined in his first sermon. The first Noble Truth is *dukkha* (literally unsatisfactoriness, but normally translated as suffering), the second is *samudhaya* (the origin of suffering, which is desire), the third is *nirodha* (the cessation of suffering, by extinction of desire) and the fourth is *magga* (the way to the cessation of suffering). To achieve the latter, the Buddha formulated what is known as the Noble Eightfold Path: right understanding, right thought or aspiration, right speech, right action, right livelihood, right effort, right mindfulness and right concentration.

The Four Noble Truths can be compared to a physician diagnosing and treating a disease. The First Noble Truth corresponds to examining a patient's symptoms: seeing suffering and noting its characteristics. The Second Noble Truth is seen as realizing the cause of the disease and reaching a diagnosis: knowing the cause of suffering. The Third Noble Truth compares to reassuring the patient of the cure: realizing that suffering can end. The Fourth Noble Truth is dispensing good advice and 'medicine': the path that leads to freedom from suffering.

It is then up to the patient to choose to take the 'medicine' or not. This is why there are two candles on the Buddhist 'altar'. They signify that a person can choose to take the path that leads to release from suffering, or choose to continue within the realm of conditioned existence.

The essence of the Buddha's teachings is succinctly expressed in the simple lines: Do good/Avoid evil/And purify the mind. The Fourth Noble Truth describes in detail how to do these, namely by following the eight components which constitute the Noble Eightfold Path. Although these components are often considered as a linear progression, the fact is that all facets of the path should be developed simultaneously. There are three main phases to the path: *sila* — morality and ethics (do good and avoid evil); *samadhi* — concentration (purify the mind); and *panna* — wisdom, which arises naturally if there is a firm base of morality, and sufficient concentration and mindfulness.

The Noble Eightfold Path, grouped under three phases, is composed of: morality — right speech, action and livelihood; concentration — right effort and mindfulness; and wisdom — right understanding and thought.

Almost all the teachings of the Buddha, conducted over a period of 45 years, connect in some way to this path. He explained them in different ways and in different words to different people, according to their level of spiritual development and capacity to understand, but the essence of the teachings in the 84,000 discourses, sermons and talks is to be found in the Noble Eightfold Path.

Buddhism explains three kinds of wisdom: the wisdom which corresponds to memorizing texts; the deeper kind of wisdom which derives from contemplating the texts; and profound wisdom, termed penetrative wisdom, which arises from integrated, intuitive experience of living. In the same way, the Four Noble Truths may be memorized and recited, they may be contemplated and discussed, or they may be experienced as interrelated facets of the experiential path to release.

Penetrative wisdom leads to an understanding of the way things are — the ultimate reality. This understanding does not arise from the accumulation of knowledge alone, it requires a clear mind, free of impurities, which can be developed through the practice of meditation.

The Sangha, the monastic order established at the time of the Buddha's first sermon, is the third part of the Triple Gem. It plays an essential role in Buddhism not only by preserving the Dhamma, but also in demonstrating to the lay community, by example. The laity supports the Sangha and, conversely, the Sangha supports the laity. This two-way relationship has helped propagate and maintain Buddhism, and has fuelled its growth. Since its establishment, the Sangha has spread throughout the East and, in recent times, to the West.

In the practice of Theravada Buddhism, the aim is to avoid evil, and lead a good life based on self-control, restraint and meditation. The laity are exhorted to observe the five basic precepts of Buddhism (abstention from killing, stealing, sexual misconduct, false speech and intoxicants), and follow the moral and ethical teachings of the Buddha. A Theravada monk is expected to adhere to 227 precepts and follow a disciplined life of devotion and service.

The laity may enter the religious order to devote more time to formal practice. Nonetheless, lay people practise in daily life, trying to maintain mindfulness and setting aside such time for more formal practice when they can.

In trying to lead a good life, everyone has the opportunity to accrue merit. The ways in which lay people may earn merit are many and various. Most typical and certainly most visible in Thailand is the giving of food and other offerings to monks as they make their early-morning alms rounds in cities, towns and villages. Commissioning the making of Buddha images, either as an individual or as part of a community, is also highly regarded as a means of making merit.

Implicit in Buddhism is an understanding of the cycle of rebirth and suffering. To end suffering, desire must be extinguished. In the Theravada tradition, cessation of desire allows a person to move towards *nibbana*, at which time the cycle of rebirth will end. Gaining merit helps to ensure rebirth under more favourable conditions, as well as better conditions in the present existence.

As with other major religions, worship plays a role in daily Buddhist practice. But whereas, for example, Christian worship involves prayer and submission to a supernatural deity, Buddhist worship is an expression of respect and gratitude to the Triple Gem: the Buddha, the Dhamma and the Sangha.

While there is no call to divine intervention in Buddhism, holding fast to the Dhamma helps to foster noble qualities such as virtue and compassion, aids purification of the mind, and improves awareness through the practice of meditation.

In common with many other religions and philosophical schools, Buddhism has evolved through different sects, or 'vehicles'. Two major ones surviving today are Theravada (the Doctrine of the Elders), and Mahayana, or 'Great Vehicle'. Theravada Buddhism is known also as *Hinayana*, or 'Lesser Vehicle'.

Though sharing basic doctrines, Theravada and Mahayana have differences stemming, in simplified terms, from the former's desire to adhere strictly to the practices followed in the days of the historical Buddha; the Mahayana school, on the other hand, wished to make some adjustments, arising to a considerable extent from the influence of pre-existing religious and cultural forms and, to a lesser extent, from needs dictated by colder climates.

The division into various schools occurred around the 1st century AD. Theravada Buddhism found a stronghold in Sri Lanka, later becoming the primary faith in Thailand, Burma, Laos and Cambodia. Mahayana Buddhism spread to China, Central Asia, Japan and other parts of East Asia, and Vietnam. Today, though still strongest in the East, Buddhism is practised internationally.

Opposite: A temple gable showing the Buddha's first sermon. Above: The Wheel of the Law, symbolizing the Buddha's teachings, was set in motion by the first sermon.

THE CENTRAL PLAINS

Stretching from the northern hills to Bangkok and the Gulf of Thailand, the Central Plains form the heart of the Kingdom, both physically and historically. It was in these fertile, plentifully watered lowlands that the Thai people became united as a nation, and where the region's large population was amply sustained by agricultural abundance.

The Central Plains are dominated by the Chao Phraya, Thailand's major river, formed by the confluence of several streams flowing down from the North. During the course of their historical development the Thais expanded the natural waterways with a network of canals which served both as irrigation channels and as communication providers for what has traditionally been a waterborne society. The flat and predominantly featureless landscape has thus been transformed into the archetypal image of Thailand, a patchwork of paddy fields from which the bulk of the country's vitally important rice crop is produced. Scattered throughout the rural scene are myriad villages as well as a considerable number of sizable towns and cities; these, together with Bangkok, the heavily urbanized and industrialized capital of Thailand, make the Central Plains the most densely populated region of the country.

To the west, the Central Plains gradually give way to hills, the tail end of the northern highlands, and the countryside presents a picture of untamed jungle and prime forest cover.

Opposite: Viewed across the town's lake at dusk, Nakhon Sawan's famous Buddha makes an impressive sight.

Intentionally constructed to catch the eye of passersby and to inspire devoutness, this golden image at Si Samrong is a striking sight on the road north from Sukhothai to Si Satchanalai.

The Si Samrong image, pictured here with familiar present-day elements, was constructed to reinforce Buddhist values in the modern age.

This Buddha in Phitsanulok is surrounded by harvested rice fields typical of the landscape of the Central Plains.

Set in tropical landscape, this scene blends key elements of Thai life and culture.

Previous pages: Monks returning from their early morning alms round, Phitsanulok. **Opposite and above:** The Buddha crowning a small hill near Taphan Hin, Phichit, serves as a reminder of the teachings for the local community.

Television aerials may dominate the skyline at Taphan
Hin **(opposite)**, but the presence of the Buddha **(above)**
and the enduring values represented by his teachings
transcend material change in the modern world.

Such is the commanding presence of the Buddha at Taphan

Hin that it provides a permanent backdrop to daily life.

The mudra of the Buddha at Taphan Hin originally
displayed the gesture of 'calling the Earth to witness',
but was later modified with the palm turned upwards
to signify charity or the granting of gifts.

*A Burmese-style reclining Buddha at Mae Sot. A student (**opposite**) chooses an appropriate position at the feet of the statue to chant from Buddhist texts in the cool of early morning.*

Previous pages: A seated Buddha gazes down on the town of Nakhon Sawan, 'Heavenly City'. **Opposite:** Viewed at night from the hills behind, and seen from the side **(above)**, the image at Nakhon Sawan is a spectacular local landmark.

This image at Nakhon Sawan sits high on a podium *(opposite)* overshadowing other statuary in the same compound, such as depicted *(above)* in this scene of the Buddha's first sermon.

Previous pages and above: *Sculpted as a bust, a Buddha
image stands out on an isolated hill near the town of Ta Khli.*

The statue near Ta Khli, viewed from the sala which enshrines a natural representation of the Buddha's footprint. It was because of the discovery of this religious symbol that the hill was originally deemed sacred.

Such is the rare size and remarkable nature of the Ta Khli bust, it has an impact as powerful as that of a full-form statue, and the image has the effect of miraculously rising from the ground.

Opposite: Looking out from a hill in Lop Buri, this Buddha is notable for its clear facial characteristics *(above)*, especially the sharply delineated eyes.

A wide variety of forms are seen in Buddhas in the open. Some closely follow traditional patterns while others, as with this image at Lop Buri, are neither classical nor strictly modern in style.

The setting sun forms a dramatic halo around the Buddha atop a hill near Lop Buri.

Opposite: Seated on Khao Phra Ngam, 'Hill of the Beautiful Buddha', in Lop Buri, this large image has been a local landmark for more than 80 years. *Above:* Detail of the face.

The statue at Khao Phra Ngam is seated below a five-tiered honorific parasol *(above)*, and gazes out over a rural landscape *(opposite)* where modern mechanized equipment is replacing some of the more traditional and arduous manual work of the past.

A panoramic view of the countryside northeast of Lop Buri town reveals a distant Buddha image on a range of hills beyond a field of sunflowers.

With an honorific parasol *(above)*, this Buddha near
Lop Buri sits amid limestone hills *(opposite)* which are
common to the area and which provide salient locations for
religious sites.

Previous pages: A huge seated Buddha rises above the trees, seemingly isolated in marshland, near Sing Buri.

Opposite: Close to, it can be seen that the statue actually sits not alone but within a temple complex. Despite the massive size of the image, the mudra (**above and right**) is expressed with delicate sensitivity.

Vehicles streak past a Buddha set beside the main highway leading from the Central Plains to the Northeast. This stretch of road has always been considered dangerous and the image was built for the purpose of offering good fortune to those who travel along it.

The grounds of Wat Phai Rong Wua, in Suphan Buri province, feature scores of Buddha images of varying size, depicting different postures and styles.

*Work on some images at Wat Phai Rong Wua, such as this huge reclining Buddha (**opposite**), has been infrequent due to lack of funds. Such delays can affect a structure's stability and, indeed, this statue's head collapsed in July 1998. The site includes Thailand's largest seated Buddha (**above**), rising to a height of over 50 metres.*

Opposite: The size of Wat Phai Rong Wua's largest and principal image is dramatically emphasized as painters climb high on scaffolding to undertake the mammoth task of restoration. *Above:* Repainting the eyes.

A Buddha image stands out atop an isolated range of hills in Ratchaburi province.

*Buddha Monthon, in Nakhon Pathom province, is one of Thailand's most famous sacred sites, built to commemorate the 2,500th anniversary of the Buddhist religion. Devotees **(right)** pay homage on Visakha Bucha Day.*

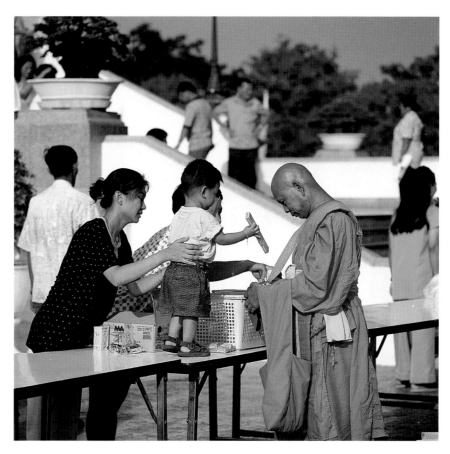

At tables laid out around the Buddha Monthon statue, monks receive alms in the early morning as part of the celebration of Visakha Bucha Day. Located close to Bangkok, the site is a popular choice for people wishing to pay homage and make merit on this and other important dates in the Buddhist calendar.

Opposite: H.R.H. Princess Maha Chakri Sirindhorn is pictured circumambulating the image on Visakha Bucha Day. *Above:* Stalls provide offerings for people to place at the base of the statue. This beautiful image is considered the finest example of Thai Buddhist sculpture in the Rattanakosin, or Bangkok, period.

*The full moon rises on the night of Visakha Bucha (**above**) as a candlelit procession (**opposite**) makes its way around the image, evoking a serene atmosphere, as experienced at many Buddhist ceremonies held on holy days in Thailand.*

Opposite: The standing image at Wat Inthara Wihan, Bangkok, is the tallest in the country to depict the Buddha with an alms bowl. It is believed that offerings made to the image *(above)* bring good fortune.

Above: *Gold leaf being applied to the toenails of the*
Wat Inthara Wihan Buddha is a token of respect.
Right: *Inner city life surrounds the temple compound.*

Left: The Buddha at Wat Inthara Wihan stands amongst Bangkok's high-rise buildings, while *(above)* those living within its immediate vicinity are afforded a striking view.

Buddhism in Thailand

The introduction of Buddhism into the part of Southeast Asia now known as Thailand predates the founding of the Kingdom by more than a thousand years. There were distinct phases of influence, including that of Mahayana and non-Buddhist Brahmanistic traditions, before Theravada Buddhism was established as the national religion.

The Thais migrated from southern China, most historians believe, and were initially animists, but in the centuries leading up to their rise to power they were exposed to Buddhism through contact with various other civilizations.

Buddhism first came to the area in the 3rd century BC when the Indian emperor Ashoka is said to have sent two missionaries to the 'Land of Gold'. This has been tentatively identified as the Mon kingdom of Dvaravati, which was centred on the modern town of Nakhon Pathom, west of Bangkok.

Later, in the 9th century AD, Mahayana Buddhism was spread by the Srivijaya kingdom, probably centred on the island of Sumatra but whose territories extended to the southern Thai peninsula. Further exposure to Mahayana Buddhism, along with Brahmanism, came some 200 years later when the Khmers of Angkor held what would later become central and northeastern Thailand. At roughly the same time, a form of Theravada Buddhism spread into the west of the country from the Burmese kingdom of Pagan.

While the seeds of Buddhism had been sown early and had come from different sources, the form that was eventually adopted by the Thais was developed from the Theravada school which had taken root in Sri Lanka.

By the time of the founding of the first Thai sovereign state at Sukhothai in the early 13th century, when both Khmer and Burmese influences were waning, Buddhist monks in southern Thailand had established firm links with Sri Lanka, and from there came the doctrine of Theravada Buddhism, based on Pali texts as opposed to the *Sanskrit* scriptures of the Mahayana vehicle.

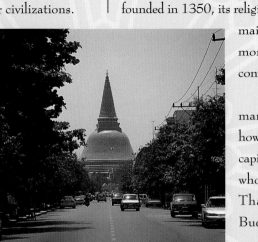

Later in that century, Sukhothai's greatest monarch, King Ramkhamhaeng (c. 1279-1298), reputedly met with southern monks, and invited them to his capital to establish Buddhism according to the Sri Lankan school. Thus supported by royal patronage and subsequent direct contact with Sri Lanka, Theravada Buddhism was embraced by the Thai nation and thrived as the religion which gave the newly united people a common bond.

When Sukhothai was eclipsed by the second Thai kingdom, Ayutthaya, founded in 1350, its religious heritage remained intact and the kings of Ayutthaya maintained the tradition of building countless temples and monasteries. Throughout Thai history royal patronage has contributed greatly to the stability and progress of Buddhism.

When Ayutthaya fell to the Burmese in 1767, many religious scripts were lost. The nation was rallied, however, first by King Taksin (1767-1782), who made a new capital at Thonburi, and then by King Rama I (1782-1809), whose power base at Bangkok became Thailand's capital. Thailand's structure and institutions survived, and Buddhism flourished as before.

The Kingdom was revitalized and modernized in the Rattanakosin period and Buddhism likewise received fresh impetus, most notably during the reign of King Mongkut, Rama IV (1851-1868). A monk for 27 years prior to ascending the throne, King Mongkut was a renowned Buddhist scholar who, in an effort to purify religious practice, created a second, stricter monastic sect, *Thammayut*. When he ascended the throne, this sect came to coexist with the traditional *Mahanikai* order, itself subjected to thorough reform.

Today, the supporting influence of the monarchy upon Buddhism in Thailand continues. Throughout his long reign, Thailand's present monarch, King Bhumibol Adulyadej, has shown, through his exemplary commitment to Buddhism, his enduring concern for the spiritual welfare of his subjects. Together with the monarchy and nationhood, Buddhism remains one of the three underpinning concepts from which Thai society draws its quintessential strength. The monastic system persists and young men still enter the monkhood for at least a brief period once in their lives, to earn merit for their parents as well as for their own spiritual development.

The monkhood serves a more active function than monastic systems in the West. In the past, when Thai society was essentially village oriented, monks would serve as teachers, doctors, counsellors and suchlike, as well as spiritual guides, and while this is less pronounced today, the multiple roles have not died out completely, particularly in rural areas where, traditionally, changes are made more slowly.

The religious community also includes *mae chi*, the approximate equivalent of nuns. Although nuns, traditionally, have enjoyed a lesser status than monks, mae chi are now accorded greater respect than in the past.

For the lay community, major Buddhist festivals are maintained as public holidays, devotees flocking to temples around the country. Chief among the celebrations are three all-important dates which commemorate significant events in the Buddha's life.

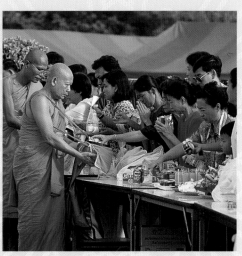

Falling on the day of the February full moon, *Makha Bucha* celebrates the occasion when 1,250 disciples gathered spontaneously to hear the Buddha speak. In May, *Visakha Bucha* celebrates the day (that of the full moon in the sixth lunar month) on which the Buddha was born, achieved enlightenment, and died. At the full moon in July, *Asalha Bucha* is the anniversary of the Buddha's first sermon to his first five disciples.

All three occasions are marked by acts of merit-making, while in the evenings crowds gather at temples and other Buddhist sites throughout Thailand, joining in candlelit processions which slowly make three circuits around the main hall or sacred structure. These celebrations, extraordinarily enhanced by the soft light of the full moon, afford scenes of remarkable serenity and quiet devotion, emphatic examples of the depth and extent of the Buddhist faith in Thailand.

Two other major occasions in the Buddhist calendar are *Khao Phansa* and *Ok Phansa* marking, respectively, the start and the end of the Rains Retreat, which is sometimes referred to, rather inaccurately, as 'Buddhist lent'. Both are variable dates, set according to the lunar calendar and occurring in July and October.

The Rains Retreat is a time when monks remain in their monasteries, devoting themselves to meditation and contemplation. The tradition predates Buddhism, and derives from ancient India where itinerant holy men would pass the rainy season in permanent dwellings lest in their wanderings they inadvertently tread on freshly planted crops. At this time, many young Thai men enter the monkhood temporarily, while lay people usually show greater religious observance and perhaps abstain from alcohol or cigarettes.

At Ok Phansa the monkhood is honoured in another traditional ceremony, *Thot Krathin*, at which time monks throughout the Kingdom are presented with new robes and various other offerings to meet their modest practical needs.

Aside from major sacred dates, each month there are four or five other *wan phra*, or 'holy days', fixed according to the moon's phases. On these days, devout Buddhists may attend a sermon at the temple or spend time in meditation.

Throughout Thailand, one other notable manifestation of Buddhism is the presence of many meditation centres. Run by monks or by lay people, they are retreats for anyone wishing to meditate for just a few days or even some months.

As one contemporary Thai commentator has remarked, 'Buddhism has become so integrated with Thai life that the two are hardly separable. Buddhist influences can be detected in Thai lifestyle, mannerisms, traditions, character, arts, architecture, language and all other aspects of the Thai culture.'

*Opposite: Phra Pathom Chedi, the world's tallest Buddhist monument, located in the centre of Nakhon Pathom. **Above:** Monks receiving alms on Visakha Bucha Day.*

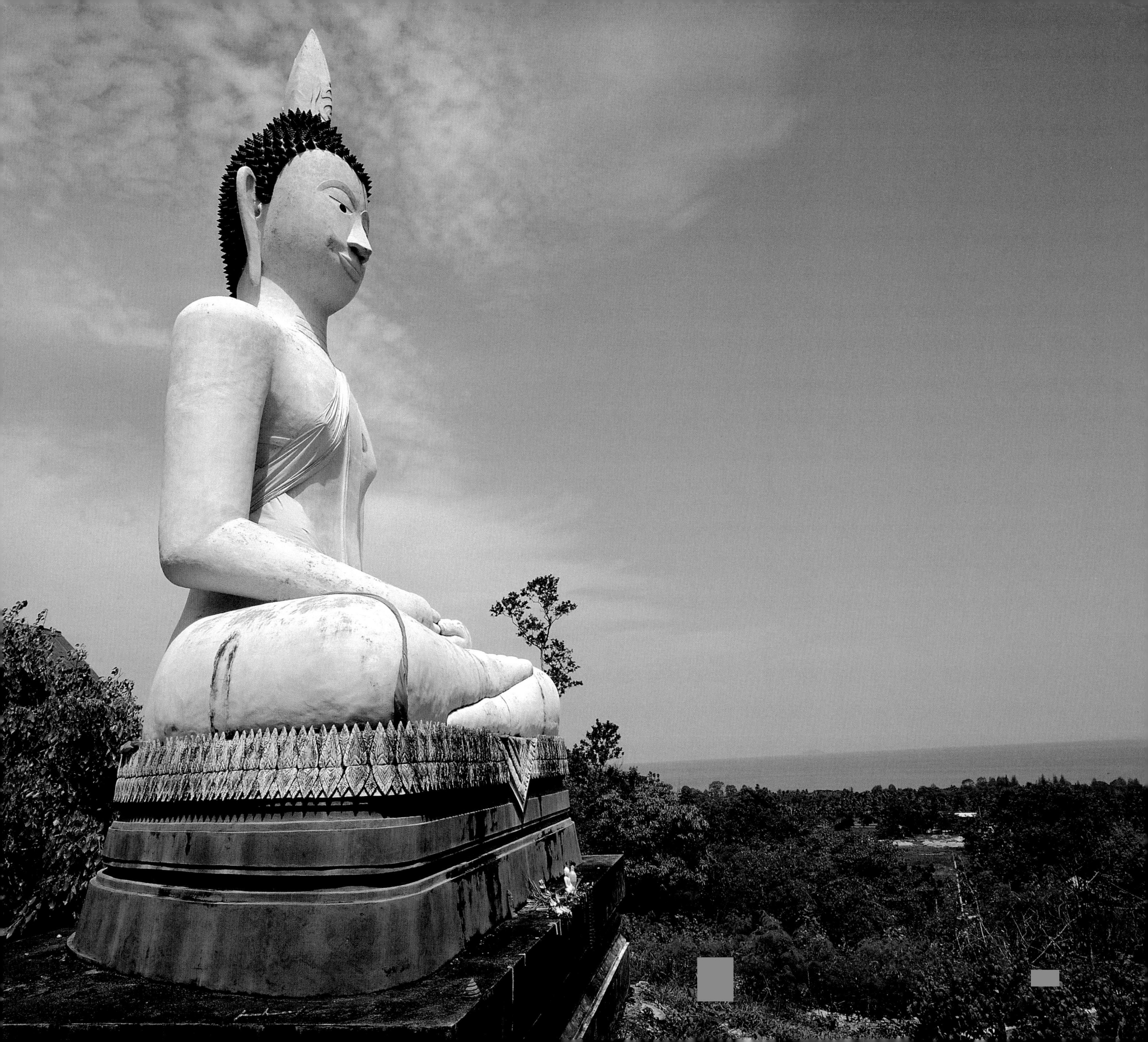

THE EAST COAST

FACING THE GULF OF THAILAND and forming an angled corner reaching some
500 kilometres from the mouth of the Chao Phraya river around to the Cambodian
border, the East Coast boasts many beaches which, along with offshore islands,
make it a natural area for seaside resorts; the biggest and most developed of these
is Pattaya.

From its early beginnings as a small fishing village, Pattaya rose quickly
to prominence during the 1960s as a rest-and-relaxation centre for United States
troops on leave from Vietnam, blossoming into a leading international holiday
destination. Today, quieter and more relaxed resorts are to be found further along
the coast in Rayong province and on the island of Koh Samet.

If it was tourism that first put the East Coast on the map, more recent fame
and prosperity are a result of the Eastern Seaboard Development Programme, a
massive infrastructure scheme involving two large industrial estates and attendant
deep-sea ports.

Away from the coast, especially in the provinces of Chanthaburi and Trat,
the area is noted for its wide variety of fresh produce, including three of Thailand's
most exotic fruits: durian, mangosteen and rambutan. Set against a backdrop of
lush green hills, this southeastern corner of the Kingdom is as a whole an extremely
attractive area whose plantations and orchards complement a natural landscape of
considerable beauty.

Opposite: On the East Coast, a seated Buddha looks out across the tropical waters of the Gulf of Thailand.

Previous pages: This Buddha in Chonburi is unusual,
seated in European style on a boat. *Above and opposite:*
A Buddha, with attendant statues, is set above the
harbour of Koh Si Chang, an island off the East Coast.

Set amid flowering shrubs, the Buddha at Koh Si Chang
commands a typical prospect of the coastal waters which
are becoming increasingly busy with port and industrial
development along the East Coast.

Above: A gold painted image crowns a hill above the built-up beach resort of Pattaya. **Opposite and left:** Away from the watersports and bustling activity for which this coastal town is famous the Buddha, amid more peaceful surroundings, offers a sense of tranquillity and solitude.

Laser-guided technology was used to etch this remarkable
Buddha image onto the rock face of Khao Chi Chan in
Chonburi province. It is the largest image of its kind in
the world.

Above and opposite: *A standing Buddha and two seated images, sited prominently above the trees, on limestone outcrops, at Wat Suk Phrai Wan in Rayong province.*

The standing Buddha at Wat Suk Phrai Wan expresses the vitarka mudra. This image clearly stands out when viewed from the surrounding flat countryside.

The Wat Suk Phrai Wan complex includes an elaborate
bridge *(above)* built to link a natural rock outcrop,
crowned by a seated Buddha, to the main hill with
its standing image *(opposite)*.

Previous pages: The main seated image at Wat Suk
Phrai Wan depicts the Buddha giving his first sermon.
Above, right and opposite: The distinctive form and
detail of a highly revered image enshrined in Phitsanulok,
the Phra Buddha Chinaraj, is reflected in this statue at
Wat Bo Thong in Rayong province.

A steep limestone hill provides the backdrop to a standing
image at Wat Rattanakhiri in Sa Kaeo province.

The Wat Rattanakhiri Buddha, set against a sheer limestone rock face, is notable for displaying a rarely depicted mudra, that of 'contemplation'.

The Making of Buddha Images

Buddha images may be fashioned from all kinds of material. Statues carved in stone, wood or crystal, shaped from terracotta, or brick and stucco, or cast in gold, silver or other metal, can all be found in Thailand. Most common are images cast in bronze, a craft in which the Thais have long excelled, although today another medium can be added to the list — reinforced concrete, the material employed for most of the large Buddhas seen in the landscape.

Modern construction materials and methods account in part for the growing number of large Buddha statues seen today; simply, they are now easier, quicker and less expensive to build than in the past, when brick and stucco were the usual materials for substantial, freestanding images. Form and function, however, are unchanging.

'People commission Buddha statues because they want to make merit. The Buddha image displays deep inner quiet, and if we want to understand life, we need to make ourselves quiet,' explains Anant Jaemjaeng, one of a handful of sculptors in Thailand who work exclusively on monumental religious statuary. He adds that the style of the statue — Thai, Chinese, Burmese or whatever — is immaterial, all Buddhas being the same in essence. Any of the traditionally established forms of the Buddha image may be used, and the choice is merely a question of the personal preference of those commissioning the statue.

'That is the first stage in the creation of a statue,' says Anant, 'asking what style or which art period should it reflect, and which form — seated, standing, walking or reclining. Once that has been decided, I draw a preliminary sketch for approval.'

A Buddhist monk for several years, Anant is a self-taught artist, learning mostly from studying Buddha images in the temple, but his accomplishment is such that he can reproduce an image in the style of any of the Thai schools of sculpture, as well as in many Chinese and other national forms.

Once the style of the statue has been approved, Anant makes scale drawings of both the statue's form and its internal structure of concrete columns reinforced with steel rods. Typically, a large freestanding Buddha image is fashioned around three main reinforced concrete columns rising from the foundations to the statue's uppermost points. These columns are then strengthened by horizontal bars which form a kind of skeleton.

Basically, the same structural technique applies to any statue, although the walking Buddha requires a more complex internal structure as the feet are not evenly placed, and so need to be 'locked' to have the strength required to support the whole statue.

In the next stage, Anant consults with a construction engineer who checks the scale drawings for structural flaws, thus always ensuring that the specified framework will have sufficient strength to support the weight of the finished statue. There have been cases where lack of attention to structural detail has led to tragic consequences: in 1997, a Buddha being built in Phitsanulok collapsed, killing three workers.

The construction engineer may make modifications to the scale drawings, but only in relation to the internal structure, not the external appearance of the image. Once the plans have been finalized, building commences with laying the foundations and erecting the reinforced concrete framework, which takes some two weeks to complete. For a statue 10 metres high (an average size, although 15-plus metres is not uncommon) another two months are needed for filling in and shaping with cement to produce the final form. Altogether, some 20-30 construction workers will be engaged on the project.

Work, however, is not always continuous. Given the costs involved — about six million baht for a 10-metre high statue — raising funds can be a long-drawn-out affair and often an image will be built in stages as money becomes available.

The overall form and proportions of a statue are dictated by the scale drawings, in which measurements are exact to the last centimetre, and the most difficult work is the actual finishing of the final shape and polished surface. Anant says that the face is a critical area, especially the eyes, as three essential characteristics of the Buddha — kindness, tranquillity and enlightenment — need to be expressed, in addition to giving the image 'life'.

Adding to the difficulty is the fact that a statue must have an impact when seen from afar. Anant explains that finalizing the face is a painstaking matter of repeatedly making small changes, then climbing down from the structure and standing back to view the work from a distance before again making minor adjustments. Lastly, but not always, the statue may be painted with oil-based paints.

Although reinforced concrete is the prime medium for modern Buddha statues standing in the open, some smaller images may be cast in bronze. To cast bronze and other metals, the Thais employ, now as in former times, what is known as the 'lost wax' process. It is a technique similar to that practised in China and the West. Two methods of the process are used, depending on whether a solid or hollow statue is to be cast. Mostly it is the size of the image that dictates the choice, large pieces requiring hollow casting for reasons of economy and technical necessity. It is, however, common to find small images which are also hollow.

In simplified terms, hollow casting requires a clay core roughly fashioned into the desired form. This is covered with a mixture of wax and shellac, of the required thickness of the finished statue (varying from little more than a millimetre to a couple of centimetres or so), and the resulting soft surface is worked to bear the features and details of the final image. The whole piece is then covered with a mould comprising three layers. First, a mixture of fine clay and other ingredients is brushed directly on to the wax model. Second and third layers comprise thick coatings of increasingly coarse clay and sand.

Once the mould is dry it is ready for casting. The whole is turned upside down and heated over a fire so that the wax melts and runs off through vents left for the purpose. Finally, molten bronze is poured into the mould, filling up the space vacated by the wax. Once the bronze has cooled and solidified, the mould is broken and thrown away.

As the mould is always destroyed and there is no difficulty in lifting it from the bronze, it is possible to cast large and intricate forms. Nonetheless, big or complicated pieces (for example, the Buddha seated under a naga) are cast as separate pieces and later assembled.

Ritual inevitably surrounds the construction of any religious object, and four main ceremonies relate to the construction of a large Buddha statue. First, at the foundation-laying stage, a ceremony known as *Long Sao Ek* celebrates the placing of the all-important first structural column; it is similar to the ritual surrounding the raising of the foundation post in traditional domestic architecture. The ceremony also involves appeasement of the spirits which are believed to occupy the land.

Next, the *Banchu Watthumongkhon* ceremony is held towards the completion of the statue and involves the placing of gold or other auspicious materials inside the image, usually in the chest or head. Both monks and lay people from the community commissioning the statue take part in the ritual, which is designed to give the image life.

When the statue is finished the *Poet Net*, or 'opening of the eyes', ceremony takes place, presided over by the King, or by a senior or highly revered monk. The celebrant places ritual powder over the eyes or forehead of the statue, signifying the image as a being rather than an object. Then, finally, the statue is blessed in a one- to three-day ceremony known as the *Chalong Sompot*.

Opposite: Sculptor Anant Jaemjaeng studies initial design drawings of a seated Buddha.
Above: Bamboo scaffolding surrounds a standing statue in the last stage of construction.

THE SOUTH

FORMING A LONG, NARROW PENINSULA, southern Thailand stretches some 1,200 kilometres from just below Bangkok to the Malaysian border. The land is characterized by a mountainous spine and humped limestone karst formations, while the coastline is indented with coves and beaches. Numerous islands, including the country's largest, Phuket, punctuate the coastal waters.

Topographically, the region divides into the upper and lower South. The upper South extends down to Chumphon, faces the Gulf of Thailand to the east and borders Myanmar to the west. Coastal settlements blend beach resorts, notably Cha-am and Hua Hin, and traditional fishing villages. Inland, cultivation on the narrow plain is dominated by plantations, particularly those of pineapple.

Beyond Chumphon, the lower South is distinguished by a more truly tropical climate and the last vestiges of Thailand's rainforests. The border with Myanmar ends near the town of Ranong, and on the western coast the Thai shore faces the Andaman Sea, while to the east the coastline adjoins the Gulf of Thailand. The landscape is dominated by rubber and coconut plantations.

Whereas the inhabitants of Thailand as a whole are overwhelmingly Buddhist, in the lower South a significant proportion of the population is Muslim.

The lower South is best known today as a resort area. Phuket island and Krabi, on the Andaman coast, and Koh Samui in the Gulf can all claim tropical beaches that rank among the finest in the world.

Opposite: This standing Buddha, which forms part of the temple complex of Wat Khao Takiap, south of Hua Hin, is a distinctive landmark on the coast.

Buddha statues may be encountered in comparatively isolated locations, as seen here on a wooded hill in the Phetchaburi countryside.

*Providing visitors to the beach resort of Hua Hin with
a visual reminder of Buddhism, the Khao Takiap image
is depicted with both hands raised in the abhaya mudra,
indicating 'calming the ocean' or 'dispelling fear'.*

The image at Khao Takiap, pictured facing a calm sea, seen in the contrasting light of sunrise *(above)* and the full moon *(opposite)*, accentuates the implicit relationship between Buddhism and nature.

Previous four pages: *A Buddha at Wat Tham Khao Tao,
near Hua Hin, is depicted in the pose of 'receiving alms'.*
Opposite: *A seated image on the coast at Wat Thang
Sai Ek in Prachuap Khiri Khan province commemorates
the 60th birthday of H.M. Queen Sirikit, in 1992, and
displays Her Majesty's royal insignia on the base* **(above)**.

Previous pages: *Making offerings and paying homage to the Buddha at Wat Thang Sai Ek on Makha Bucha Day.* **Above:** *The image at dawn and* **(opposite)** *detail of the face.*

Previous pages, opposite and above: A huge Buddha image in Chumphon province sits amongst the hills, dominates the landscape, and is readily visible from the surrounding countryside.

Above: *The Buddha at Chumphon rises above the* *treetops.* ***Opposite:*** *Aspects of the image in detail.*

Previous pages: *The image popularly known as 'The Big Buddha' is Koh Samui's most sacred coastal landmark.*
Above: *A steep naga-flanked stairway leads to the statue (right), the face of which (opposite) is a modern rendering of classical styles.*

Opposite: In Songkhla province, a large Buddha, seated beneath a naga, forms a striking backdrop to school playing fields. *Above:* Viewed from the front, the statue is contrasted by an attendant image.

A reclining Buddha in the Mae Lan district of Pattani province, an image which serves as a constant reminder of Buddhist teachings to the children at the adjacent village school.

Sunset over the statue of Phra Buddha Thaksin Ming Mongkhon in Narathiwat province.

Lit by the morning sun, the golden image stands out against the lush green environment of Narathiwat.

Opposite: *Devotees regularly pay homage to this robust image in Narathiwat, set in the predominantly Muslim area of Thailand's far south.* **Above:** *Detail of the face.*

Expressing a gracefully sculpted mudra *(above)*, the
Narathiwat image *(opposite)* so clearly illustrates the
powerful impact of Buddha statues in the landscape
and the sacred expression of Thailand that they project.

Additional Captions

The North

pages 32, 72-73

Phra Buddha Chomket Maha Mangkhalanuson King Rama IX.
Wat Phra That Chom Wae, Amphur Phan, Chiang Rai province.
Located on a hill close to Phan, approx. 1 km west of Highway 1, 45 km south of Chiang Rai. Chiang Saen style. Approx. 18 m high. Built 1994.

pages 34-35

Phra Buddha Thanaphi Siphingkharat.
Wat Phra That Doi Kham, Amphur Muang, Chiang Mai province.
Located on Doi Kham, approx. 5 km southwest of Chiang Mai airport. Chiang Saen, Phra Singh style. 16 m high. Built 1988.

pages 36-41

Phra Buddha Maha Patimakorn Thira Uthai Panyasupa Sammasarn Buddha Chao.
Wat Doi Saket, Amphur Doi Saket, Chiang Mai province.
Located on the hill of Doi Saket, close to Highway 118, 14 km north of Chiang Mai. Mix of Chiang Saen, Sukhothai and U-Thong styles. Approx. 14 m high. Built 1992-97.

pages 42-43

Phra Buddha Mongkhon.
Wat Phra Non, Amphur Muang, Mae Hong Son province.
Located in the centre of Mae Hong Son. Burmese style. Approx. 8 m high.

pages 44-47

Phra Buddha Siri Pracha Nakha Banphot (gold Buddha) and Luang Pho Yai (white Buddha).
Wat Tha Ton, Amphur Mae Ai, Chiang Mai province.
Located in temple grounds on a hill close to the Myanmar border, in Tha Ton, overlooking the Mae Kok river, approx. 180 km north of Chiang Mai on Highway 107. Gold Buddha: Approx. 12 m high to the top of the naga. Built 1989, following a dream in which the person who commissioned the image saw a Buddha glittering in the sky, holding out a round golden glass. White Buddha: Chiang Saen style. Approx. 14 m high. Built 1984, by donations from Bangkok, to provide protection and good luck for the town.

pages 48-49

Phra Buddha Luang Poet Lok.
Kittilak Dhamma Park Meditation Centre, Amphur Muang, Chiang Rai province.
Located in the hills surrounding Chiang Rai, approx. 10 km northwest of the town. 11 m high to the top of the tiered honorific parasol. Built 1989.

pages 50-55

Unnamed Buddha image at Wat Phra That Chom Mok Kaeo, Amphur Mae Lao, Chiang Rai province.
Located close to the secondary road that links Chiang Rai to Highway 118, approx. 35 km heading southwest from Chiang Rai. Approx. 7 m high. Built 1995.

front cover, pages 56-57

Phra Buddha Ong Luang (Luang Pho Buddha Ong Yonok Ming Mongkhon Chiang Saen).
Wat Phra That Chom Kitti, Amphur Chiang Saen, Chiang Rai province.
Located just off the Chiang Saen bypass road, approx. 3 km from town, travelling west towards the Golden Triangle. Approx. 10 m high.

pages 58-59

Phra Buddha Yonok Rattana Mongkhon.
Wat San That Asokaram, Amphur Chiang Saen, Chiang Rai province.
Located in the wooded temple grounds of Wat San That Asokaram, approx. 9 km east of the main road between Mae Chan and Chiang Saen. The turning is on the left, 3 km south of Chiang Saen. 15 m high. Built 1976. The statue commemorates the story from the Buddha's life when, while in retreat in the Parileyyaka Forest, he was venerated and assisted by a lone monkey and an elephant. In return, the Buddha offered the animals rebirth into the realm of Indra, who showed them the way to salvation. This tale is extremely popular as it illustrates the good that comes to all beings who make contact with the Buddha. A multitude of animal sculptures are to be found amongst this leafy glade surrounding the Buddha. They were built to serve as a reminder for people to live together in harmony with the animal kingdom.

pages 60-63

Phra Buddha Sing 1, Doi Tone.
Doi Tone Meditation Centre, Amphur Mae Chan, Chiang Rai province.
Located on a small hill, 1 km south of the Mae Chan - Tha Ton road, 3 km from Mae Chan, which lies 28 km north of Chiang Rai. Approx. 18 m high (including base). Built 1995-98. The image contains objects of silver and gold, and gemstones.

back cover, pages 64-65

Unnamed Buddha image at Wat Ban San Phattana, Amphur Mae Chan, Chiang Rai province.
Located on the side of a hill, 1 km southwest of the Mae Chan - Tha Ton road, 2 km from Mae Chan. Chiang Saen style. 24 m long. Built 1993.

pages 66-67

Phra Buddha Saksi Chom Mueng.
Wat Phra That Chom Cho (Wat Phra Borom That Chom Cho), Amphur Thoeng, Chiang Rai province.
Located on a hillside to the south of the road, just before reaching the town of Thoeng, 56 km southwest of Chiang Rai. Approx. 17 m high. Built 1993.

pages 8, 68-69

Phra Buddha Ong Luang.
Wat Phra That Pong Klua, Amphur Chiang Muan, Phayao province.
Located west of the main road, approx. 15 km from the village of Pong, on the way to Chiang Muan, approx. 50 km east of Phayao. Approx. 12 m high. Built 1994.

pages 70-71

Phra Buddha Udom Mongkhon.

Wat Udom Wari, Amphur Phan, Chiang Rai province.

Located in temple grounds, approx. 1 km east of Highway 1, 30 km south of Chiang Rai. 17 m high. Built 1986.

pages 74-79

Phra Buddha Leela.

Wat Analayo Tiphayaram, Doi Busarakam, Amphur Muang, Phayao province.

Located on a hill in the temple complex, 10 km west of Phayao, 95 km south of Chiang Rai via Highway 1. Chiang Saen style. Bronze weighing 254 tonnes. 25 m high. Built 1992-1998 to commemorate the 50th anniversary of H.M. the King's accession to the throne. The location was chosen by the abbot, who had a vision of a halo of bright golden light surrounding the hill. After practising vipassana meditation, the abbot had a further dream of a large Buddha standing on the hill.

pages 80-83

Luang Pho Phra Chao Ong Luang.

Wat Phra That Nong Chan, Amphur Song, Phrae province.

Located on level ground at Wat Phra That Nong Chan, 2 km east of Highway 103, approx. 15 km from Rong Kwang, 32 km northeast of Phrae. Lanna style. Approx. 15 m high. Built 1979-1993.

The Northeast

pages 86, 88-93

Phra Buddha Sakon Sima Mongkhon.

Wat Thep Phithak Punnaram, Amphur Pak Chong, Nakhon Ratchasima province.

Located on the side of a hill, 3 km south of Highway 2, approx. 40 km east of Saraburi. Construction was begun by a highly respected abbot named Phra Sutthitham Rangsi Methachan who believed the site was sacred, as well as being the main gateway to the Northeast, and wanted to make an image of the Lord Buddha seated in the open. He died before his vision was fulfilled, and the work was completed by his followers. Approx. 40 m high. Built 1969.

pages 7, 94-99

Phra Buddha Uttara Maha Mongkhon Ubonrat.

Wat Phra Bat Phu Phan Kham, Amphur Ubonrat, Khon Kaen province.

Located on a hill between the town and Ubonrat reservoir. Ubonrat is 15 km west of Highway 2, and approx. 45 km northwest of Khon Kaen. Constructed by an abbot from Samut Prakan who returned each year to Ubonrat to pay respect to his ancestors. Approx. 40 m high. Built 1970-75.

pages 100-101

Luang Pho Buddha Saiyat Pha Cho.

Wat Tham Pha Cho, Amphur Ubonrat, Khon Kaen province.

Located approx. 4 km from Ubonrat, on the east side of the small road leading to fishing villages by the reservoir. The natural rock formation was seen as the most notable natural feature in the landscape and hence a suitable site for a Buddha statue. The image is especially revered by people suffering from serious illness. Approx. 10 m long. Built 1963.

pages 102-105

Phra Buddha Chaiyasi.

Wat Tham Erawan, Amphur Na Klang, Nong Bua Lam Phu province.

Located on the side of a hill, 4 km north of Highway 210, approx. 80 km west of Udon Thani. Approx. 13 m high. Built 1979.

pages 106-107

Phra Buddha Si Sukhot Wangka Banphot Sathit Nara Nora Buchit Udom Khuna.

Wat Tham Pha Wang, Amphur Na Klang, Nong Bua Lam Phu province.

Located on Highway 210, approx. 80 km west of Udon Thani. Approx. 15 m high. Built 1994-97.

pages 108-109

Phra Buddha Chao Yai.

Wat Buddha Banphot (Wat Tham Pha Cho Thepnimit), Amphur Na Klang, Nong Bua Lam Phu province.

Located on a hill, 1 km south of Highway 210, approx. 65 km west of Udon Thani. This hill attracts many visitors because of its fine natural features. The Buddha was built on the hill for visitors to pay homage. Approx. 7 m high. Built 1969.

pages 110-111

Unnamed Buddha image at Wat Phithak Watthanaram, Amphur Muang, Nong Bua Lam Phu province.

Located in the hills, approx. 8 km south of Highway 210, approx. 42 km west of Udon Thani. The turn-off from Highway 210 is some 5 km before Nong Bua Lam Phu. Approx. 12 m high. Uncompleted.

pages 112-113

Unnamed Buddha image at Amphur Tha Bo, Nong Khai province.

Located in fields between a minor road and the banks of the Mekong river, approx. 15 km west of Nong Khai. Approx. 7 m high (including the nine-tiered honorific parasol). Origin unknown.

pages 14, 114-115

Somdet Phra Boromma Trai Lokanat.

Wat Noi Pho Kham (Wat Phra Yai), Amphur Muang, Nakhon Phanom province.

Located on the outskirts of Nakhon Phanom. 36 m high. Built 1984-86.

pages 116-119, 139

Luang Pho Thammachak.

Wat Phu Dan Tae (Wat Buddha Thammatharo), Amphur Nikhom Kham Soi, Mukdahan province.

Located on the west of Highway 212, 55 km north of Amnat Charoen, near Nikhom Kham Soi. For novice monks attending the Buddhist school in the temple grounds, the Buddha provides a constant visual reminder of the teachings. Approx. 15 m high. Built 1976.

pages 120-121

PHRA MONGKHON MING MUANG.

BUDDHA UTTHAYAN KHAO DAN PHRA BAT, AMPHUR MUANG, AMNAT CHAROEN PROVINCE.

Located in a park on the west of Highway 212, 3 km north of Amnat Charoen. Small ancient clay Buddhas and other sacred objects were found in the area, suggesting a temple may have previously stood on the site which has now been developed into a park and place for vipassana meditation. Sacred relics are enshrined in the image, which is patterned after the Indian Pala style. Approx. 18 m high (including base). Built 1965.

inside front cover, pages 1, 122-127

PHRA BUDDHA RATTANA MONGKHON MAHA MUNI.

WAT BURAPHAPHIRAM, AMPHUR MUANG, ROI ET PROVINCE.

Located in the centre of Roi Et. The image is covered in small mosaic tiles. 67.85 m high. Built 1979.

pages 128-129

PHRA PHROM BHUMIPALO.

PHU SINGH BUDDHIST MONASTERY, AMPHUR SAHATSAKHAN, KALASIN PROVINCE.

Located on Khao Phu Singh, a hill close to the Lam Pao reservoir, approx. 32 km north of Kalasin, along the road adjacent to the reservoir. Kalasin is 70 km east of Khon Kaen. Approx. 12 m high. Built 1968.

pages 130-131

PHRA SUPHATTHARA BOPHIT.

KHAO KRADONG, AMPHUR MUANG, BURI RAM PROVINCE.

Located on Khao Kradong, a hill off Highway 218, approx. 6 km south of Buri Ram. Approx. 18 m high.

pages 132-137, 278-279

PHRA BUDDHA SURIN MONGKHON.

WAT PHANOM SILA KHAO SAWAI, AMPHUR MUANG, SURIN PROVINCE.

Located on Khao Sawai, a hill approx. 22 km south of Surin, which is 40 km east of Buri Ram. The hill is traditionally a site of pilgrimage for the local community during Songkran, the Thai New Year festival, in April. 30 m high. Built 1975-77.

The Central Plains

pages 140, 156-161

PHRA SI SUKHOT SAWAN.

WACHIRAKANLAYA MONASTERY, AMPHUR MUANG, NAKHON SAWAN PROVINCE.

Located on a slight rise overlooking Nakhon Sawan, on the north side of the town. 23 m high. Built 1982.

pages 142-143

PHRA SUKHOTHAI ONG YAI.

WAT SOPHARAM, AMPHUR SI SAMRONG, SUKHOTHAI PROVINCE.

Located on the west of Highway 101, approx. 20 km north of Sukhothai town. Constructed to reinforce Buddhist values in the modern age. Sukhothai style. 28 m high. Built 1995.

pages 144-147, 280

SOMDET PHRA BOROMMA LOKACHET WISUTTHIYA SATTHA THEWA MANUSANANG.

WAT KHLONG RUA, AMPHUR WANG THONG, PHITSANULOK PROVINCE.

Located approx. 500 m south of Highway 101, 18 km east of Phitsanulok. The statue was constructed after the abbot dreamt that some spirits gave him a lotus, requesting him to build a large Buddha image as it would assist their path to heaven. 24 m high. Built 1993.

pages 148-149

LUANG PHO PRATHANPHON.

WAT KHAO PHRA, AMPHUR MUANG, PHICHIT PROVINCE.

Located on a small hill at the village of Baan Khao Phra, 1 km north of the main road, 15 km south of Phichit, on the route to Taphan Hin, approx. 65 km south of Phitsanulok. Constructed for the local community. 13 m high. Built 1965-68.

pages 150-153

PHRA BUDDHA KETMONGKHON.

WAT THEWAPRASAT, AMPHUR TAPHAN HIN, PHICHIT PROVINCE.

Located in the centre of Taphan Hin, approx. 80 km south of Phitsanulok. 24 m high. Built 1970.

pages 154-155

PHRA NON SAMAKKHI.

WAT THAI WATTHANARAM, AMPHUR MAE SOT, TAK PROVINCE.

Located at Mae Sot, which lies on the border with Myanmar. Burmese style. Approx. 45 m long. Built 1994-96.

pages 10-11, 162-167

PHRA BUDDHA KETKAEO CHULA MANI.

WAT THAM PHUKHA, AMPHUR TA KHLI, NAKHON SAWAN PROVINCE.

Located on an isolated hill, Khao Phukha, 10 km north of Ta Khli, which is approx. 20 km west of Highway 1 and approx. 60 km southeast of Nakhon Sawan. The history of the site dates back to the reign of King Rama VI (1910-25) when engineers constructing the nearby northern railway line wanted to use rock from the hill. Their efforts to blast the rock were continually thwarted by inexplicable events, and when King Rama VI heard of this he designated the hill a natural resource which should be protected. The subsequent discovery of a Buddha footprint, after villagers had several times seen a strange golden light on the hill, led to the site being considered sacred and appropriate for construction of a large Buddha statue. An airforce base was located close by and the size of the image had to be restricted in order not to interfere with the flight path. Accordingly, it was decided to make the image in the form of a bust so as to maintain size and impact while restricting height. Approx. 13 m high.

pages 168-171

PHRA BUDDHA MONGKHON NIMIT.

WAT KHUHA SAWAN, AMPHUR MUANG, LOP BURI PROVINCE.

Located on a rock outcrop, approx. 10 km east of Lop Buri. Approx. 10 m high. Built 1973.

pages 12, 172-175

Luang Pho Phra Ngam (Phra Buddha Patiphak Mattayom Buddhakan).

Wat Khao Phra Ngam (Wat Siri Chantaranimit Wora Wihan), Amphur Muang, Lop Buri province.

Located on Khao Phra Ngam, 'Hill of the Beautiful Buddha', on Highway 1, approx. 15 km north of Lop Buri. Approx. 35 m high. Built 1912.

pages 176-179

Phra Buddha Tham Rangsi Muninat Satsada Suphamatsadu.

Wat Weluwan Khao Cheen Lae, Amphur Muang, Lop Buri province.

Located in rocky hills, 3 km west of the road that runs north from Highway 1 to Phatthana Nikhom. The turning off Highway 1 is approx. 10 km east of Lop Buri, and the path into the hills is approx. 10 km along the turn-off. Chiang Saen style. Approx. 12 m high. Built 1973.

pages 180-183

Phra Buddha Suwan Mongkhon Maha Muni.

Wat Phikun Thong, Amphur Tha Chang, Sing Buri province.

Located approx. 15 km south of Sing Buri, off Highway 311. Sukhothai influence; covered in gold mosaic tiles from Italy. Approx. 30 m high. Built 1974.

pages 184-185

Phra Buddha Prapat Muni.

Wat Sap Bon, Amphur Kaeng Khoi, Saraburi province.

Located on Highway 2, 30 km east of Saraburi. Constructed by a previous abbot,

following a dream in which three people gave him lotus buds which bloomed and revealed a large Buddha image. 20 m high. Built 1961-1972.

pages 186-191

Phra Buddha Kakusantho.

Wat Phai Rong Wua (Wat Photharam), Amphur Song Phi Nong, Suphan Buri province.

Located 15 km west of Highway 340. The turning is approx. 40 km south of Suphan Buri. The site comprises an array of statues, including a gigantic seated Buddha, over 50 m high, and a huge, as yet unfinished, reclining Buddha. Construction progress of the latter was halted in July 1998 due to the collapse of the statue's head. The temple complex contains statuary depicting episodes from the Buddha's life, as well as scenes from heaven and hell. Indian-style monuments representing important holy sites have also been constructed in the temple grounds.

pages 192-193

Unnamed Buddha image at Amphur Pak Tho, Ratchaburi province.

Located on a rocky hill, approx. 4 km west of Highway 4, 20 km south of Ratchaburi. Approx. 12 m high.

pages 194-199

Phra Si Sakkaya Thotsaphonyan Prathan Buddha Monthon Suthat.

Buddha Monthon, Amphur Buddha Monthon, Nakhon Pathom province.

Located in a landscaped park, approx. 35 km to the west of Bangkok, along

Highway 338 and 15 km east of Nakhon Pathom town. The park is planted with a variety of trees and shrubs mentioned in Buddhist history. The image of the walking Buddha is in Rattanakosin, or Bangkok, style and displays a fine modern interpretation of the classical Sukhothai form. In 1982, H.R.H. Maha Chakri Sirindhorn attended the Chalong Sompot ceremony for the image. Members of the Royal Family regularly attend religious ceremonies here on important dates in the Buddhist calendar. 15.8 m high. Built 1980-1982.

pages 200-203

Luang Pho To (Phra Si Ariya Mettrai).

Wat Inthara Wihan, Amphur Phra Nakhon, Bangkok.

Located in the subdistrict of Bangkhunphrom. 32 m high. Built 1867-1927. In 1964 and 1967, Their Majesties the King and Queen of Thailand applied gold leaf to the statue's topknot and forehead, while in 1978 H.R.H. Crown Prince Vajiralongkorn presided over a ceremony to place, in the topknot of the image, holy relics presented to Thailand by the government of Sri Lanka. In 1982, to commemorate the bicentennial of Bangkok becoming the capital of Thailand, 24 kt gold mosaic tiles from Italy were applied to the statue. The image is believed to possess miraculous powers. Offerings made to the Buddha, especially the head of a mackerel, a boiled egg and a flower garland, are thought to bring good fortune.

The East Coast

page 206

Unnamed Buddha image at Wat Khao Bamphenboon, Amphur Sattahip, Chonburi province.

Located on a hill, east of Highway 3, some 15 km south of Pattaya. Approx. 10 m high.

pages 208-209

Phra Buddha Mongkhon Nimit.

Wat Thamma Nimit, Amphur Muang, Chonburi province.

Located in temple grounds on a hillside overlooking Chonburi. The statue, seated European style on a boat, represents an episode in the Buddha's life when he returned to visit his father and had to cross a lake on the way. Two tones of mosaic tiles cover the image. The robes, in darker tone, feature tiles from Japan whereas the lighter tiles of the skin come from Italy. 32 m high. Built 1974 to replace an earlier image constructed in 1956.

pages 210-213

Ong Si Suk Maha Chakraphet.

Tham Chakrapong Monastery, Amphur Koh Si Chang, Chonburi province.

Located on the offshore island of Koh Si Chang, a 40-minute ferry ride from Si Racha, approx. 20 km south of Chonburi. Covered in mosaic tiles. Approx. 12 m high. Built 1983.

pages 214-215

Phra Buddha Sukhothai Walai Chonlathan.
Wat Phra Buddha Yai, Amphur Muang Pattaya, Chonburi province.
Located on a hill, just south of Pattaya. Painted gold and surrounded by smaller attendant statues. Approx. 12 m high. Built 1977.

pages 216-217

Phra Buddha Maha Vajira Uttamophat Satsada.
Amphur Bang Lamung, Chonburi province.
Etched onto the rockface of Khao Chi Chan, approx. 6 km north of Highway 3 from the turning some 13 km south of Pattaya. The area around Khao Chi Chan has been developed as a public park, landscaped with plants and trees mentioned in Buddhist history. The laser guided technology used to carve the image was supervised by the Asian Institute of Technology. 150 m high. Built in 1996 to commemorate the 50th anniversary of H.M. the King's accession to the throne.

pages 218-225

Than Pho Yai Chaiya Mongkhon Muni Sisanphet Boromma Lokanat Satsadachan Phichit Man Prathanphon (Standing Buddha).
Wat Suk Phrai Wan, Amphur Klaeng, Rayong province.
Located on a hill in temple grounds, approx. 3 km south of Highway 3, approx. 60 km east of Rayong. The style of the statues was influenced by visits the temple abbot made to India, and the statues were built to help promote protection of the local environment. Standing Buddha, 16 m high. Built 1977.

pages 226-227

Phra Buddha Chinathep.
Wat Bo Thong, Amphur Klaeng, Rayong province.
Located on a hill, south of Highway 3, approx. 45 km east of Rayong. Approx. 14 m high. Built 1995.

pages 228-229

Unnamed Buddha image at Wat Rattanakhiri, Amphur Wang Nam Yen, Sa Kaeo province.
Located on a hill, east of Highway 317, approx. 145 km north of Chanthaburi. Approx. 15 m high. Built 1973.

The South

pages 232, 236-239

Unnamed Buddha image at Wat Khao Takiap, Amphur Hua Hin, Prachuap Khiri Khan province.
Located near the sea, at the foot of Khao Takiap, approx. 10 km south of Hua Hin. The mudra indicates 'calming the ocean' or 'dispelling fear', reflecting the abbot's belief that faith in Buddhism promotes peace. Approx. 17 m high. Built 1983.

pages 234-235

Luang Pho Yai.
Wat Khao Phra Phrom Cha Ngae, Amphur Ban Lat, Phetchaburi province.
Located on a small hill, 2 km east of Highway 4, 15 km south of Phetchaburi. 13 m high. Built 1960.

pages 240-243

Ong Pathom Samma Sam Buddha Chao.
Wat Tham Khao Tao, Amphur Hua Hin, Prachuap Khiri Khan province.
Located close to the sea on the side of Khao Tao, a hill approx. 20 km south of Hua Hin. Depicted in the posture of receiving alms, this image is believed to attract good fortune. 10 m high. Built 1990.

pages 244-249

Phra Buddha Kitti Sirichai.
Wat Thang Sai Ek, Khao Thong Chai, Amphur Bang Saphan, Prachuap Khiri Khan province.
Located on a hill, near the sea, approx. 60 km south of Prachuap Khiri Khan. The statue contains sacred relics of the Buddha, presented by the Supreme Patriarch, which were enshrined during a ceremony presided over by H.R.H. Princess Maha Chakri Sirindhorn in 1996. Approx. 10 m high. Built 1990-93.

pages 2-3, 250-255, 276-277

Phra Buddha Yai.
Wat Khao Chedi Wisai Trairattanaram, Amphur Muang, Chumphon province.
Located on a hill, to the west of Highway 41, approx. 25 km south of Chumphon. In addition to being a reminder of the teachings of the Lord Buddha, the statue was built to offer protection to travellers. Approx. 40 m high. Foundation stone laid 1968, completed 1993.

pages 4-5, 256-259

Phra Buddha Yai.
Wat Hin Ngu, Amphur Koh Samui, Surat Thani province.
Located on Koh Fan, a small rocky islet connected to the northern coast of Koh Samui by a causeway. The statue is set within the temple complex, which includes a meditation centre offering tuition to Thais and foreigners alike. 12 m high. Built 1972.

pages 260-261

Unnamed Buddha image at Wat Nang Lao, Amphur Sathing Phra, Songkhla province.
Located to the west of Highway 408, approx. 5 km north of Sathing Phra, which is approx. 60 km north of Songkhla. Approx. 30 m high from base to top of naga. Built 1986.

pages 262-263

Unnamed Buddha image at Wat Buppha Nimit, Amphur Mae Lan, Pattani province.
Located approx. 30 km west of Pattani, some 5 km from the famous temple of Wat Chang Hai. 27 m long. Built 1976.

pages 264-269

Phra Buddha Thaksin Ming Mongkhon.
Wat Khao Kong, Amphur Muang, Narathiwat province.
Located on a small hill in a park, approx. 6 km west of Narathiwat. Southern Indian style. His Majesty King Bhumibol Adulyadej presided over the 'opening of the eyes' ceremony in 1970. 24 m high, covered in gold mosaic tiles. Built 1966-69.

abhaya mudra *gesture of 'dispelling fear', figure usually standing (see page 236)*

achaan *respectful title for a teacher*

amphur *district or administrative region within a province*

amphur muang *central district of a provincial capital, i.e. Amphur Muang for Chiang Mai province would be the central district of Chiang Mai city*

Asalha Bucha *one of the three most holy days in the Buddhist calendar, being the anniversary of the Buddha's first sermon to his first five disciples*

Banchu Watthumongkhon *the ceremony, just before completion of a new Buddha statue, in which auspicious objects are placed within the image*

bhikkhu *originally, a disciple of the Buddha; latterly, a Buddhist monk*

bhumisparsa mudra *gesture of 'calling the Earth to witness', known also as 'subduing Mara', seated figure; symbolizes when Mara (the god of temptation) was defeated trying to tempt the Buddha away from enlightenment (see page 114)*

bodhi *or* **bo** *ficus religiosa: the tree under which the Buddha attained enlightenment while meditating*

Bodhisattva *a being on the path to enlightenment; in Theravada, a future Buddha; in Mahayana, one who renounces Buddhahood, out of compassion, to aid the liberation of all living beings*

Brahman *a Hindu priest*

Buddha *'The Enlightened One', or 'The Awakened One'; the title by which Siddhattha Gotama became known after having become fully enlightened*

Chalong Sompot *the ceremony, after completion of a new Buddha statue, in which the image is blessed*

chedi *stupa; monument erected to house sacred Buddhist relics*

Dhamma *or* **Dharma** *the teachings of the Buddha; Buddhist law*

dhammacakra mudra *gesture of 'setting the Wheel of Law in motion', seated figure (see page 119)*

dhyana mudra *gesture of meditation, seated figure (see page 63)*

doi *mountain*

dukkha *suffering or unsatisfactoriness*

Hinayana *see* ***Theravada***

khao *hill*

Khao Phansa *a holy day in the Buddhist calendar, marking the start of the Rains Retreat in July*

koh *island*

Long Sao Ek *the ceremony, at the foundation-laying stage of building a new Buddha statue, celebrating the placing of the first structural column*

luang pho *venerable father; honorific title for an abbot*

mae chi *Thai Buddhist nun*

magga *way to the cessation of suffering*

Mahanikai *the major Thai monastic order*

Mahayana *the form of Buddhism practised in China, Central Asia, Japan and elsewhere in East Asia, and Vietnam; also known as 'the Greater Vehicle'*

Makha Bucha *one of the three most holy days in the Buddhist calendar, commemorating the occasion when 1,250 disciples gathered spontaneously to hear the Buddha speak*

mondop *square-plan building used to house a Buddha image or other holy object*

mudra *a hand gesture which indicates a particular activity associated with a historic moment in the Buddha's life*

naga *a mythical serpent of great wisdom*

nakhon *city*

nibbana *or* **nirvana** *the ultimate truth; the ultimate reality; after enlightenment, the final liberation from the cycle of death and rebirth*

nirodha *the cessation of suffering, by extinction of desire*

Ok Phansa *a holy day in the Buddhist calendar, marking the end of the Rains Retreat in October*

Pali *an ancient language of India, derived from Sanskrit, used in Theravada holy writings*

panna *wisdom*

parinibbana *the death of the Buddha; the final passing away of a completely enlightened being, never to be reborn*

phra *an honorific title for a Buddha image or a monk*

Poet Net *the ceremony, when the building of a new Buddha statue has been completed, at which the 'opening of the eyes' takes place, symbolizing the image as a being rather than an object*

samadhi *concentration*

samudhaya *the origin of suffering, which is desire*

Sangha *the monastic order founded by the Buddha*

Sanskrit *an ancient language of India, used in Mahayana holy writings; the language from which Pali was derived*

sila *morality*

sutta *Buddhist text or discourse*

teja *the fiery intellectual energy which the Buddha reputedly possessed in abundance*

tham *cave*

Thammayut *a strict Thai monastic order founded by King Mongkut, emphasizing the disciplines of meditation and learning*

Theravada *the form of Buddhism practised in Thailand, Myanmar, Cambodia, Laos, and Sri Lanka; the 'Doctrine of the Elders'; also known as Hinayana, or 'the Lesser Vehicle'*

Thot Krathin *a holy period following Ok Phansa, when new robes and other offerings are presented to monks*

Triratna *the Triple Gem, comprising the Buddha, the Dhamma and the Sangha*

usnisa *cranial protuberance on the head of the Buddha, one of 32 major marks associated with his physical appearance*

varada mudra *gesture of giving or charity, seated or standing figure (see page 67)*

vipassana *insight*

Visakha Bucha *the most holy day in the Buddhist calendar, celebrating the day, in the sixth lunar month, on which the Buddha was born, achieved enlightenment, and died*

vitarka mudra *gesture of reasoning or giving instruction, seated or standing figure (see page 40)*

wai *the traditional Thai greeting and departure salutation, palms of the hands pressed together, held in front of the chest*

wan phra *the term for a Buddhist holy day in Thailand*

wat *a Thai Buddhist monastery*

yai *big*

Further Reading

Bechert, Heinz, & Gombrich, Richard, editors, **The World of Buddhism**, London, Thames & Hudson, 1984.

Boisselier, J., **The Heritage of Thai Sculpture**, translated by J. Emmons, New York & Tokyo, Weatherhill, 1975.

Boisselier, Jean, **The Wisdom of the Buddha**, translated by Carey Lovelace, London, Thames & Hudson, 1994.

Bowie, Theodore, editor, **The Arts of Thailand**, Bloomington, Indiana University, 1960.

Buribhand, Luang Boribal, & Griswold, A.B., **Thai Images of the Buddha**, Bangkok, Fine Arts Department, 1980.

Diskul, Professor M.C. Subhadradis, **Art in Thailand: A Brief History**, fifth edition, Bangkok, Amarin Press, 1981.

Fickle, Dorothy H., **Images of the Buddha in Thailand**, Singapore, Oxford University Press, 1989.

Griswold, A.B., **What Is a Buddha Image?** Bangkok, Fine Arts Department, 1974.

Hoskin, John, **Buddha Images in the Grand Palace**, Bangkok, Office of His Majesty's Principal Private Secretary, 1994.

Humphreys, Christmas, **Buddhism**, Harmondsworth, Penguin Books, 1951.

Khantipalo Bhikkhu, **Buddhism Explained**, revised edition, Chiang Mai, Silkworm Books, 1989.

Krairiksh, Piriya, **The Sacred Image: Sculptures from Thailand**, Cologne, Museum for East-Asian Art, 1979.

Krairiksh, Piriya, **Sculptures from Thailand**, Hong Kong, Urban Council, 1982.

Matics, K.I., **Gestures of the Buddha**, Bangkok, Chulalongkorn University Press, 1998.

Plamintr, Sunthorn, **Getting to Know Buddhism**, Bangkok, Buddhadhamma Foundation, 1994.

Powell, Andrew, **Living Buddhism**, London, British Museum Publications, 1989.

Rahula, Venerable Dr. W., **What the Buddha Taught**, Bangkok, Haw Trai Foundation, 1988.

Rajadhon, Phya Anuman, **Popular Buddhism in Siam and Other Essays on Thai Studies**, Bangkok, Thai Inter-Religious Commission for Development, and Sathirakoses Nagapradipa, 1986.

Rajanubhab, Prince Damrong, **Monuments of the Buddha in Siam**, second edition, Bangkok, Siam Society, 1973.

Roscoe, Gerald, **The Good Life: A Guide to Buddhism for the Westerner**, Bangkok, Asia Books, 1990.

Van Beek, Steve, **The Arts of Thailand**, Hong Kong, Travel Publishing Asia, 1985.

Woodward, Hiram W., Jr., **The Sacred Sculpture of Thailand**, London, Thames & Hudson, 1997.

Acknowledgements

The photographer would like to thank the following who provided valuable assistance during the preparation of *Buddha in the Landscape:*

To those companies and organizations whose support has made this book possible: Tourism Authority of Thailand; Thai Airways International; Dusit Hotels and Resorts; Nation Multimedia Group; Nu Life International (Thailand); The Peninsula Plaza; Vongvanij Foundation; and Format and Partners.

For their professional advice: Professor M.C. Subhadradis Diskul; M.R. Usnisa Sukhsvasti; Achaan Jayasaro; Achaan Sujib Punyanubhab; Anurut Vongvanij; Achaan Helen Jandamit; Dr. Suvit Yodmani; Suangsuda Sopapun; Trungjai Itharat; and Dr. Duangtip Surintatip.

During production: Keith Hardy, for his editing and valuable advice; John Hoskin; Annie Miniscloux; Kris Gomeze; Sommit Barpuyawart; Disraporn Yatprom; Frederik Hardvendel; Juergen Gutzeit; Napavee Thippayasak; Thomas and Katie Burke; James Donnelly; Dr. Rapin Tongra-ar; Mana Prapassarangkul; Hiran Shacatanont; Kelvin Lai; and Alice Chua.

To those who assisted me on location: Siripong Siriluck; Peerach Doets Mhaitong; Mark Hassan; and Wannapa Thippayasak.

To the people who provided other invaluable assistance: Than Phra Achaan Phaibun Sumangalo; Uthon Plueangwichathon; Phruek Rangkhawara; the abbots at the many temples visited; staff at T.A.T. offices in Bangkok, Udon Thani, Ayutthaya, Nakhon Phanom and Ubon Ratchathani, for being so helpful; staff at Ayutthaya Historical Park; Buatim Hardy; the Junchompoo family; the Thippayasak family; the Siriluck family; the Nathalant family; Kitti Chongphithatana; Pensupa Gajeseni Darakananda; Robert Speechley; Sheila Hulbert; Payap Boonmark; Veera Simaroj; Cherdsak Chawanapreecha; Seri Matthanimabura; Anant Jaemjaeng; the management of the Star Beach Condotel, Pattaya; and the management of Dhevi Mansion, Bangkok.

Last, but not least, for their enduring support and understanding throughout the project: my mother Marjorie; my wife Nai; and my son Jack.

Phra Buddha Surin Mongkhon at Wat Phanom Sila
Khao Sawai, Surin province.

THE PHOTOGRAPHY

All photographs were taken using Hasselblad 503CXi, Horseman SW612, Linhoff Technorama 6 x 17 and Leica R6 cameras. The film stock employed was primarily Kodak Ektachrome 100 PLUS and Fuji Fujichrome Astia 100 professional colour reversal film. These were chosen for their natural colour performance in harmony with the subject matter, each type used for specific light conditions.

Nearly all the photographs were taken with the camera mounted on a sturdy tripod, especially when using a 1000 mm lens equivalent (500 mm mirror lens with a doubler) on the R6. High-power telephoto lenses were invaluable when photographing Buddha images from distances of several kilometres, such as for the photograph on page 171.

The photography included planning certain pictures in relation to the course of the sun and, sometimes, the ideal angle would only be right after waiting many months. This often involved returning to the location several times to monitor the sun's position on the horizon in order to judge the optimum moment to capture the scene.

All the photographs were taken without using any special effect filters or multiple exposure techniques.